An Illustrated History of

EXMOOR'S RAILWAYS

Minehead shed above in 1935 and opposite in the early 1950s - sub to Taunton the shed closed in November 1956. There were occasions when Minehead had an allocation of two engines, but during most of the early 1950s the usual resident(s) were '2251' class 0-6-0s. The '45XX' 2-6-2Ts monopolised Minehead's lists from 1927 to 1943 and, to the best of my limited knowledge, no '51XXs' were ever actually stabled there. Therefore, the two engines seen opposite - Nos 5554 and 5185 - were unlikely to have been official residents. PHOTOS: W.A.CAMWELL and TERRY NICHOLLS

Mortehoe and Woolacombe station, 21 July 1964. The SRs 'N' class 2-6-0s were regular performers on the Ilfacombe line, No.31837 being in charge of the 5.15pm Barnstaple Junction to Ilfracombe train. PHOTO: ROGER PALMER

An Illustrated History

of

EXMOOR'S RAILWAYS

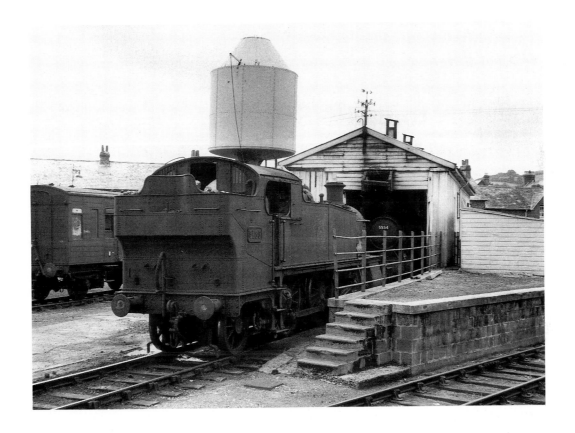

By
Martin Smith

IRWELL
PRESS

Contents

TAUNTON to MINEHEAD

The West Somerset Railway - the Minehead Railway -
GWR days and after .... **Page 3**

TAUNTON to BARNSTAPLE

The Devon & Somerset Railway - the GWR - connections to Barnstaple .... **Page 24**

BARNSTAPLE to ILFRACOMBE

The L&SWR outpost - Barnstaple shed - the 'ACE' and the 'Belle' .... **Page 44**

THE LYNTON & BARNSTAPLE RAILWAY

Teething troubles - SR ownership - an early demise .... **Page 58**

THE WEST SOMERSET RAILWAY

Ore traffic - then passenger services - but a very early end .... **Page 72**

First Published in the United Kingdom by
IRWELL PRESS 1995
P.O.Box 1260, Caernarfon, Gwynedd, LL55 3ZD
Printed in Huddersfield by The Amadeus Press

INTRODUCTION

In the early 1960s, Taunton's '61XX' 2-6-2Ts saw reasonably regular usage on the Minehead branch. In this classic WR branch line snap, No 6148 approaches Washford with the 9.45am Minehead -Taunton train, on 22 August 1964. As if to make the title of this book seem misleading, the hills in the background are the Brendons, not Exmoor. PHOTO: M.J. FOX

I readily admit that this book strays a little beyond the true geographical confines of Exmoor. Nevertheless, I hope this does not detract from a modest look at the railways of one of the South West's most attractive corners. This book devotes a separate section to each of the area's five railway lines and, fortunately for the sake of variety, no less than four different railway companies were involved in their development. All five lines have previously been well documented elsewhere, and so this book is *NOT* an attempt to provide further allegedly-definitive histories. That said, considerable primary source research has been undertaken in an effort to come up with something a little different, and it is hoped that the end result provides a brief - and sometimes off-beat - insight into contemporary railway operations in the West Somerset and North Devon areas.

Martin Smith, Coleford, Somerset. June 1994.

ACKNOWLEDGEMENTS

It would be wholly unfair for me to try to claim the credit for every scrap of detail contained in this book. A wealth of information and constructive advice was provided by Mr Eric Youldon of Exeter and Mr Bill Peto of the Great Western Society, to whom very sizeable 'thank-yous' are due for their invaluable contributions. Welcome assistance was also forthcoming from Hugh Ballantyne, Mr D. Bromwich (Somerset Local History Library), Chris Hawkins, George Reeve, the staff at the West Country Studies Library, Exeter, and, despite their notorious new computer system, the staff at the Public Record Office, Kew. Last, but definitely not least, sincere thanks are due to my wife, Micky, who tells me that her patience is without parallel. I'll not argue.

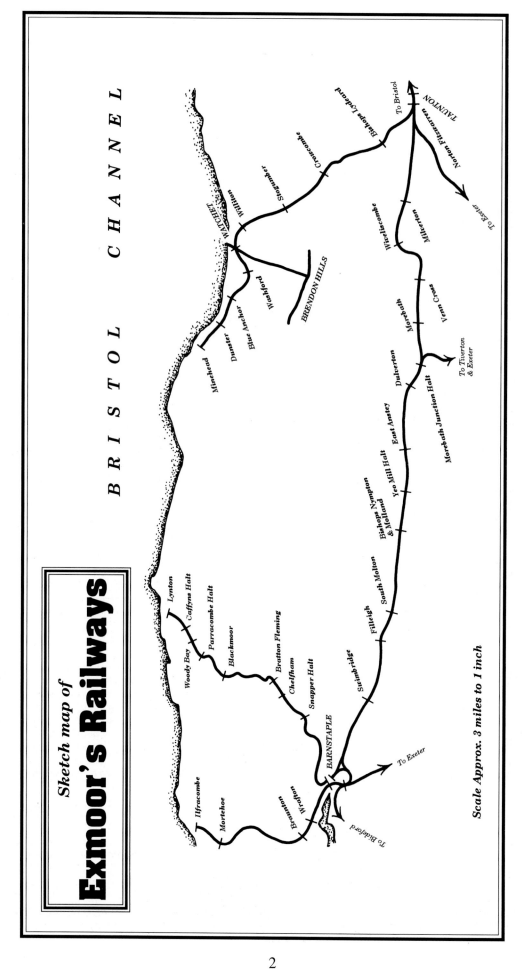

Sketch map of
Exmoor's Railways

BRISTOL CHANNEL

Scale Approx. 3 miles to 1 inch

Lynton
Caffyns Halt
Woody Bay
Parracombe Halt
Blackmoor
Bratton Fleming
Chelfham
Snapper Halt

Ilfracombe
Mortehoe
Braunton
Wrafton

BARNSTAPLE
To Exeter
To Bideford

Swimbridge
Filleigh
South Molton
Bishops Nympton
& Molland
Yeo Mill Halt
East Anstey
Dulverton
Morebath Junction Halt
To Tiverton
& Exeter
Morebath
Venn Cross
Milverton
Wiveliscombe

Minehead
Dunster
Blue Anchor
Washford
WATCHET
Williton
Stogumber
Crowcombe
Bishops Lydeard

BRENDON HILLS

To Bristol
TAUNTON
Norton Fitzwarren
To Exeter

TAUNTON to MINEHEAD

The branch Line from Taunton to Minehead was completed by two separate companies, and was worked by an entirely different concern. That state of affairs was, however, not so much a comment on the closeness between the various companies, but more a reflection of the financial necessities of Victorian railway enterprise.

The West Somerset Railway was incorporated on 17 August 1857 to construct a 141/2 mile line from Norton Fitzwarren (near Taunton) to the harbour at Watchet. Nominally, Isambard Kingdom Brunel was the engineer, but matters were effectively overseen by his assistant, Robert Brereton, who formally succeeded Brunel after the latter's death in 1859. Promoted mainly by local landowners, the WSR soon found itself in the financial mire and was subsequently leased by the Bristol & Exeter Railway - a working agreement with the B&ER had already been arranged and the line was, consequently, built to the broad gauge. The terms of the B&ER's lease were a relatively modest 45% of gross receipts, but subject, initially, to a minimum of £4,500

pa. The minimum figure, incidentally, increased to £5,100 pa by 1871 and to £6,000 pa for 1876 onwards.

The WSR's customary entry in 'Bradshaw's Shareholders' Guide' actually made the company's financial position sound quite satisfactory. The 1869 entry, for example, announced that: *'The receipts for the six months ending the 30th June (1868) were £3,397, as compared with £3,077 in the corresponding half of 1867, showing an increase of £320. In the twelve weeks between the 28th June and 20th September (1868) the receipts were £2,666, while in the corresponding twelve weeks of 1867 they had been £2,128, showing an increase of £138. The minimum rental for the six months, after payment of the interest on the debenture bonds, left a balance of £1,247 applicable to the payment of a dividend on the first issue of 5,220 preference shares and of the current expenses. A dividend at the rate of 41/2 per cent per annum on the 5 per cent dividend shares was declared'.* The four and a half per cent dividend might sound modest, but for the same year the Great Western Railway paid less than one and a half per cent.

The line was inspected for the Board of Trade by Captain (later Colonel) Rich, who made his report on 17 March 1862. *'I had previously inspected this railway on the 7th inst, but could not report it complete in consequence of there being no lodges at the level crossings, and several minor points unfinished........ the width*

BISHOP'S LYDEARD					
	STAFF		RECEIPTS (£)		
Year	No.	Wages	Pass	Goods	Total
1903	3	148	1268	2851	4119
1913	4	226	1280	3508	4788
1923	5	703	2186	4742	6928
1924	5	745	1995	3891	5886
1925	5	733	1972	4362	6334
1926	5	643	1846	4247	6093
1927	5	657	1710	5033	6743
1928	6	730	1451	4228	5679
1929	6	822	1276	5267	6543
1930	6	889	1126	5077	6203
1931	6	832	895	4238	5133
1932	5	768	819	3539	4358
1933	5	773	761	4462	5223

An archetypal GWR branch line scene from the inter-war period? Not quite. This was Bishop's Lydeard station on 30 June 1991, the superb restoration work having been undertaken by the 'new' West Somerset Railway. PHOTO: AUTHOR

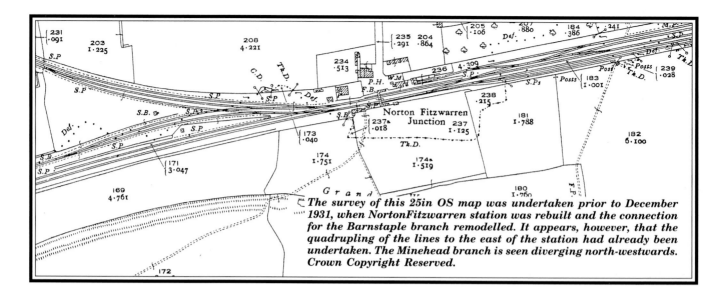

The survey of this 25in OS map was undertaken prior to December 1931, when Norton Fitzwarren station was rebuilt and the connection for the Barnstaple branch remodelled. It appears, however, that the quadrupling of the lines to the east of the station had already been undertaken. The Minehead branch is seen diverging north-westwards. *Crown Copyright Reserved.*

of the line at formation level is 17 feet in cuttings and 21 feet on embankments. The Bridge rail, in lengths of 18 feet and 20 feet, weighing 62lb per lineal yard, is fixed to longitudinal sleepers 12in by 6in with transoms. The ballast is in some cases gravel, in others broken stone and shingle - its average depth is 1ft 6in.

'There are eleven over-bridges of various spans, from 13ft to 6ft 6in —one of these has cast iron girders, the rest are constructed of masonry and brick. Seventeen under-bridges of spans from 14ft 4in to 50 feet — four of these have wrought iron girders, the rest are built of stone, brick and mortar. The whole of the bridges are well and substantially constructed.

There are two public level crossings - one at 7m 55ch (from Norton Fitzwarren Junction) and the other at 8m 36ch. The gates close across the railway. Distant signals as well as discs and lamps on the gates are provided. The lodges for the gate-keepers, which were not commenced when I inspected the line on the 7th, are now built of brick to a height of about 7ft, and will be completed before the end of the month. An engine turntable is provided at Watchet and another at Taunton'.

That was good enough for Captain Rich, and permission to open was granted. The single track line (Taunton station to Watchet - 16¾ miles) opened to passenger traffic on 31 March 1862.

	CROWCOMBE				
	STAFF		RECEIPTS (£)		
Year	No.	Wages	Pass	Goods	Total
1903	4	203	862	598	1423
1913	4	223	913	969	1882
1923	4	461	1643	2121	3764
1924	4	483	1783	3483	5263
1925	4	571	1650	3439	5089
1926	4	526	1356	3699	5055
1927	4	583	1289	3746	5035
1928	4	561	1022	2605	3627
1929	4	515	966	2495	9461
1930	4	512	956	1812	2768
1931	4	535	850	3623	4473
1932	4	485	720	1918	2638
1933	4	449	595	2206	2801

Crowcombe station, looking east towards Norton Fitzwarren, September 1964. The start of the 1 in 81 gradient at the Up end of the station is evident. *PHOTO: ANDREW MUCKLEY*

Bradshaw's 1874. The Watchet - Minehead section opened on 16 July of that year.

WEST SOMERSET. — Bristol and Exeter.							Up.						1, Station for Porlock, Lynmouth, Lynton, Ilfracombe, &c.
Miles	*From Bristol &c., see p.8.*	1&2	1,2,3,	1&2	1&2	1&2		1,2,3	1&2	1&2	1&2	1&2	
	BRISTOL 3 ......dep	6 15	8 10	12 30	3 15	6	Minehead........dep	8 30	11 20	2 35	5 43	8 15	
	Taunton ....dep	8 20	11 15	2 30	5 40	8 10	Dunster ...."	8 36	11 26	2 41	5 51	8 21	
2	Norton Fitzwarren	8 25	11 20	2 35	5 45	9 15	Blue Anchor ...."	8 43	11 33	2 48	5 58	8 28	
5	Bishop's Lydeard ...."	8 39	11 27	2 43	5 52	8 22	Washford............."	8 52	11 42	2 57	7	8 37	
9	Crowcombe Heathfield ..	8 48	11 41	2 56	6	8 36	Watchet ...."	9 6	11 59	3 5	6 15	8 45	
11¾	Stogumber	8 53	11 48	3 3	6 13	8 43	Williton ...."	9 6	11 57	3 12	6 22	8 52	
15	Williton	9 6	11 57	3 12	6 22	8 5	Stogumber ...."	9 19	12 10	3 25	6 35	9 5	
16¾	Watchet	9 14	12 5	3 20	6 30	9 0	Crowcombe Heathfield.."	9 26	12 17	3 32	6 42	9 12	
19¾	Washford...........	9 22	12 13	3 28	6 39	9 8	Bishop's Lydeard ....."	9 34	12 25	3 40	6 50	9 20	
21	Blue Anchor	9 31	12 22	3 37	6 47	9 17	Norton Fitzwarren ...."	9 45	12 36	3 51	7 1	9 31	
23	Dunster	9 39	12 30	3 45	6 55	9 25	Taunton < 3 ... ..."	9 5	12 41	3 56	7 6	9 36	
24¼	Minehead 1 ....arr	9 44	12 35	3 50	7 0	9 30	BRISTOL 6 ....arr	11 40	2 3	6 30	9 50	12 33	

The goods sheds were not ready until August, but some goods traffic is known to have been carried before the end of June - it has been suggested that this was 'van goods' conveyed by passenger trains. The intermediate stations were at Bishop's Lydeard (5 miles from Taunton station), Crowcombe Heathfield - renamed Crowcombe on 1 December 1889- (9 miles) Stogumber (11¾ miles), and Williton (15 miles). Norton Fitzwarren station, on the main Taunton - Exeter line just before the point where the branch diverged, was added on 1 August 1873.

Watchet was a sensible target for a railway as, in the late 1850s, the town's harbour had been greatly improved for the West Somerset Mineral Railway (more of which later). The two companies - the WSR and the WSMR - carried on with their own separate spheres of activity at Watchet, the WSR concentrating on imports which included coal, wood pulp from Scandinavia and esparto grass from North Africa.

The facilities for importing coal at Watchet attracted applications for the establishment of coal depots, the Chairman of the WSR and the Watchet Harbour Board, Sir Alexander Acland Hood, writing on the subject to the B&ER's Chairman, Lord Devon, on 29 March 1870:

'Two applications have been sent (from Thomas Griffiths and John Brogden & Sons) for Coal Depots near the low level lines at Watchet Station and Harbour, and I find that the most convenient site for the said Coal Depots would be a portion of the Ground now let to Mr John Thorne, Timber Merchant, Watchet, who rents of your Company the greatest portion of an otherwise unoccupied space between the low level lines for the purpose of depositing his Timber........ I beg to urge most earnestly on your Board, and on you as Chairman, that this application be acceded to, and I am sure you will see that it is only fair that the West Somerset Railway should have every opportunity of

Crowcombe station, looking east, circa 1910. The old bridge rails through Crowcombe station were not replaced until 1924. This period picture provides a nice comparison with the previous one, the gas lamps on the platforms being among the various subtle changes to the station architecture and fitments. PHOTO: JOHN SMITH

Stogumber station, looking towards Norton Fitzwarren, late 1950s. A camping coach was a feature of the station from the late 1930s until 1964 - the final season of camping coaches on the WR. One point of interest is that until the early 1920s, Stogumber had a signal box. It was located roughly where the platform bench is seen in this picture. PHOTO: JOHN L SMITH

developing their Coal Traffic, on which the future prosperity of the Line so much depends. I have invested upwards of Seventy Thousand Pounds in the Line, and I am most anxious for my own interest as well as for that of the other Shareholders

that every effort should be made to develop the Traffic of the Line'.

Among the many surviving WSR documents are minutes of a Director's meeting of 15 January 1870, which mention a letter received from the Bristol

& Exeter Railway's Secretary: 'I have laid before my Directors the offer in your letter of 10th Instant to sell to this Company for £140 the Cottage and Part of Ground adjoining Stogumber Station (owned by the WSR), now occupied by Booking

---

GWR Working Timetable, October 1886.

MINEHEAD BRANCH.

NARROW GAUGE.

Single Line worked by Train Staff. The Staff Stations are Norton Fitzwarren, Williton, Watchet, and Minehead.

Section.	Form of Staff and Tickets.	Colour of Ticket.
Norton Fitzwarren and Williton	Square	Red.
Williton and Watchet	Triangular	White.
Watchet and Minehead	Round	Blue.

Down Trains.   TAUNTON TO MINEHEAD.   Week Days only.

Miles from Taunton	STATIONS.	1 Goods. arr.	1 Goods. dep.	2 Passenger. arr.	2 Passenger. dep.	3 Goods. arr.	3 Goods. dep.	4 Passenger. arr.	4 Passenger. dep.	5 Passenger. arr.	5 Passenger. dep.	6 Passenger. arr.	6 Passenger. dep.	7 Passenger. arr.	7 Passenger. dep.	8	9
		A.M.	A.M.	A.M.	A.M.	A.M.	A.M.	A.M.	A.M.	P.M.	P.M.	P.M.	P.M.	P.M.	P.M.		
	Taunton....		6 20		8 0		10 5		11 30		1 55		4 10		7 0		
2	Norton Fitzwarren	6 26	6 40	8 4	8 5	10 11X	10 25	11 34	11 35	1 59	2 0	4 14	4 15	7 4	X7 5		
2¼	Norton Siding																
5	Bishop's Lydeard																
9	Crowcombe	6 55	7 0	8 14	8 15	10 40	10 48	11 44	11 45	2 7	2 8	4 24	4 25	7 14	7 15		
11¾	Stogumber	7 25	7 35	8 26	8 27	11 3	11 10	11 56	11 58	2 18	2 19	4 35	4 36	7 26	7 28		
15	Williton	7 45	7 55	8 33	8 31	11 19	11 27	12 3	12 5	2 24	2 25	4 41	4 42	7 33	7 35		
16¾	Watchet	8 6	8 15	8 41	8 43	11 38	X12 25	12 13	X12 16	2 31	X2 33	4 49	X4 51	7 42	X7 44		
19	Washford	X8 20		8 48	X8 49	12 32	12 39	12 19	12 20	2 38	2 39	4 55	4 56	7 48	7 49		
21¼	Blue Anchor			8 55	8 56	12 47	12 52	12 26	12 27	2 45	2 46	5 2	5 3	7 55	7 56		
23	Dunster			9 2	9 3			12 32	12 33	2 51	2 52	5 9	5 10	8 1	8 2		
24¾	**Minehead**			9 8	9 10	1 6	1 13	12 38	12 40	2 58	3 0	5 16	5 16	8 6	8 8		
				9 15		1 20		12 45		3 5		5 20		8 13			

A Runs on Saturdays only.

CROSSING ARRANGEMENTS BETWEEN NORTON FITZWARREN AND MINEHEAD.

The 6.20 a.m. Train from Taunton will cross the 8.10 a.m. Train from Minehead at Watchet.

The 8.0 a.m. Train from Taunton will cross the 8.10 a.m. Train from Minehead at Williton, and the 8.55 a.m. Train from Watchet at Watchet.

The 10.5 a.m. Train from Taunton will cross the 8.55 a.m. Train from Watchet at Norton Fitzwarren; the 11.45 a.m. Train from Minehead at Williton, and shunt for the 11.30 a.m. Train from Taunton, at Williton.

The 11.30 a.m. Train from Taunton will cross the 11.45 a.m. from Minehead, and pass the 10.5 a.m. Train from Taunton at Williton.

The 1.55 p.m. Train from Taunton will cross the 2.0 p.m. Train from Minehead at Williton.

The 4.10 p.m. Train from Taunton on Saturdays will cross the 3.40 p.m. Train from Minehead at Williton.

The 7.0 p.m. Train from Taunton will cross the 5.50 p.m. Train from Minehead at Norton Fitzwarren, and on Saturdays it will cross the 7.10 p.m. Train from Minehead at Williton.

GWR Working Timetable

Up Trains. MINEHEAD TO TAUNTON. Week Days only.

Miles from Minehead.	STATIONS.	1 Passenger. arr.	1 Passenger. dep.	2 Goods. arr.	2 Goods. dep.	3 Passenger. arr.	3 Passenger. dep.	4 Passenger. arr.	4 Passenger. dep.	5 Goods. arr.	5 Goods. dep.	6 Passenger. arr.	6 Passenger. dep.	7 A Passenger. arr.	7 A Passenger. dep.	8	8	9	9
		A.M.	A.M.	A.M.	A.M.	A.M.	A.M.	P.M.	P.M.	P.M.	P.M.	P.M.	P.M.	P.M.	P.M.				
	Minehead	....	8 10	....	....	....	11 45	....	2 0	....	3 40	....	5 50	....	*7 10*	....	....	....	....
1¾	Dunster	8 14	8 15	..	..	11 48	11 49	2 3	2 4	3 46	3 51	5 54	5 55	*7 14*	*7 15*	..	..	..	..
3½	Blue Anchor	8 20	8 21	....	....	11 54	11 55	2 9	2 10	—	—	6 0	6 1	*7 20*	*7 21*	....	....	....	....
5¾	Washford	8 28	8 29	..	..	12 3	12 4	2 17	2 18	4 5	4 10	6 8	6 9	*7 28*	*7 29*	..	..	..	..
8	Watchet	8 34	X8 36	....	X8 55	12 9	12 10	2 23	2 24	4 17	4 27	6 16	6 17	*7 35*	*7 36*	....	....	....	....
9¾	Williton	8 41	X8 44	9 0	9 5	12 15	X12 18	2 29	X2 32	4 32	X4 50	6 22	6 25	*7 42*	X*7 44*	..	..	..	..
13	Stogumber	8 52	8 54	9 14	9 20	12 26	12 27	2 39	2 40	4 59	5 4	6 33	6 34	*7 52*	*7 53*	....	....	....	....
15¾	Crowcombe	9 3	9 4	9 29	9 34	12 35	12 36	2 47	2 48	5 13	5 18	6 42	6 43	*8 1*	*8 2*	..	..	..	..
19¾	Bishop's Lydeard	9 12	9 13	9 44	9 49	12 42	12 43	2 53	2 54	5 28	5 33	6 49	6 50	*8 8*	*8 9*	....	....	....	....
22¼	Norton Siding	—	—	—	—	—	—	—	—	C.	R.	—	—	—	—	..	..	..	..
22¾	Norton Fitzwarren	9 22	9 24	9 59	X10 25	12 49	12 51	2 59	3 1	5 48	6 0	6 56	X6 58	*8 14*	*8 17*	....	....	....	....
24¾	**Taunton**	9 29	..	10 30	..	12 56	..	3 5	..	6 5	..	7 3	..	*8 22*	..	..	..	..	..

A Runs on Saturdays only.

CROSSING ARRANGEMENTS BETWEEN MINEHEAD AND NORTON FITZWARREN.

The 8.10 a.m. Train from Minehead will cross the 6.20 a.m. Train from Taunton at Watchet, and the 8.0 a.m. Train from Taunton at Williton.

The 8.55 a.m. Train from Watchet will cross the 8.0 a.m. Train from Taunton at Watchet, and the 10.5 a.m. Train from Taunton at Norton Fitzwarren.

The 11.45 a.m. Train from Minehead will cross the 10.5 a.m. and 11.30 a.m. Trains from Taunton at Williton.

The 2.0 p.m. Train from Minehead will cross the 1.55 p.m. Train from Taunton at Williton.

The 3.40 p.m. Train from Minehead will cross the 4.10 p.m. Train from Taunton on Saturdays at Williton.

The 5.50 p.m. Train from Minehead will cross the 7.0 p.m. Train from Taunton at Norton Fitzwarren.

The 7.10 p.m. Train from Minehead on Saturdays will cross the 7.0 p.m. Train from Taunton at Williton.

	STOGUMBER				
	STAFF		RECEIPTS (£)		
Year	No.	Wages	Pass	Goods	Total
1903	3	142	791	1102	1893
1913	3	144	869	1405	2274
1923	3	427	1331	1079	2410
1924	3	406	1272	1044	2316
1925	3	460	1206	1074	2280
1926	3	364	1179	1046	2225
1927	3	367	1030	1164	2194
1928	3	369	932	928	1860
1929	3	402	910	863	1773
1930	3	373	751	899	1650
1931	3	368	716	674	1390
1932	3	369	765	653	1418
1933	3	455	749	486	1235

Porter Stokes. The premises having been inspected, it appears from the Report received that the roof, which is of thatch, is in bad condition, the wet coming through in several places and requires either to be entirely new thatched or the thatch roof taken off and replaced by a tile roof, at a cost of from £15 to £20. The Directors are advised that the sum of £140 would be beyond its value in its present condition and in addition to the necessary repairs or fresh roofing, but if your Company will put on the new roof in substantial manner, my Directors would purchase the Cottage etc for the sum named, or they will do the necessary work if your Company will allow £20 for the same in the Purchase Money, which would then be £120 for the Premises as they stand'.

A thatched cottage in West Somerset for just treble the average working man's annual income?? Try finding one these days - even with a leaking roof - for a similar amount!

It appears that the WSR and the B&ER did not see eye-to-eye about various aspects of the operation and management of coal traffic and, furthermore, the disparity in the charging for coal traffic was a specific bone of contention. A report (dated 19 December 1869) on the state of play was presented to the WSR's directors at the same meeting of 15 January 1870. One topic under scrutiny was that *'In respect to Watchet, Mr Griffiths offered to provide*

Stogumber station, looking towards Minehead, September 1964. Despite its relatively recent coat of paint, the goods shed had ceased to handle public traffic since August the previous year. The stone building on the right was the goods office, earlier pictures published elsewhere showing it to have had a taller and even more substantial chimney, on the apex of the roof. PHOTO: ANDREW MUCKLEY

Williton station, looking west towards Minehead, possibly early 1900s. When compared with some of the other views of the station, the style of the footbridge, the permanent way, the gas lamps, and the wooden Up platform are the most readily identifiable differences. PHOTO: JOHN L SMITH

and work a Steam Crane for unloading Coal from the Vessels into the Waggons, and to haul the loaded waggons from the East Pier to the Main Line, for the sum of sixpence per ton; and that offer was accepted by the Harbour Commissioners. Of course it was within the province of the Harbour Commissioners to provide and pay for the hauling of the waggons to the Main Line, as this service properly appertained to the Bristol and Exeter Com-

pany, and should have been performed at their cost, nevertheless, the arrangement seems to have been generally acquiesced in, or at any rate was unchallenged till Mr Griffiths made a demand on the Bris-

tol and Exeter Company for a further two pence per ton, and about the 1st November ultimo, that Company agreed to pay, and are now paying him two pence a ton for hauling the loaded waggons to the

WILLITON					
	STAFF		RECEIPTS (£)		
Year	No.	Wages	Pass	Goods	Total
1903	4	200	2057	2237	4294
1913	4	281	1958	2691	4649
1923	4	635	2668	4557	7225
1924	4	651	2677	5573	8250
1925	4	652	2704	5610	8314
1926	4	624	2762	5890	8652
1927	4	691	2795	5171	7966
1928	4	691	2299	4563	6862
1929	4	682	2068	4681	6749
1930	4	625	1997	4490	6487
1931	4	650	1875	3758	5633
1932	5	742	1615	5161	6776
1933	4	587	1756	3876	5632

Williton station, looking south towards Norton Fitzwarren, September 1964. This is, of course, the same station as in the previous picture, but note the different track alignment at the far end of the Up platform, the footbridge and a water crane, and the 40mph speed marker beyond the end of Up platform (15mph on the previous picture). The site behind the Down platform (on the right) is now the diesel headquarters of the preserved West Somerset Railway. PHOTO: ANDREW MUCKLEY

Williton station, looking west, late 1870s. Although this picture has appeared in print countless times before, no apologies are offered for using it yet again. Rumours that the train was a special excursion for local water board employees can, however, be discounted. The engine and train are operating on the broad gauge, the locomotive seemingly a Bristol & Exeter 4-4-0ST.
PHOTO: LENS OF SUTTON

Main Line. It is therefore clear that Mr Griffiths is receiving double payment for one service.

Mr Griffiths will doubtless assert that the sixpence per ton did not pay him, but he volunteered to do the work at that rate.

The charge for unloading from the Vessels into the waggons should be the same at Watchet and Bridgwater (the latter being used by the B&ER itself); and as the charge at the latter port is now fourpence per ton, that at Watchet should at once be

made the same. The hauling to the Main Line at both places being now performed and paid for by the Bristol and Exeter Railway Company, the two Ports would then be in all respects on equal terms as to rates and facilities'.

It was suggested that: 'Mr Wall, as Agent of the Bristol and Exeter Company, provides and works the Steam Cranes at Bridgwater Wharf; and it would, to a great extent, prevent misunderstanding and disputes if an arrangement could be

entered into with him to work the Watchet Cranes on the same terms as those at Bridgwater'.

A rather more magnanimous observation was that: 'In reference to the suggestion that the low and middle level lines at Watchet should be worked by Locomotives, I am of opinion that, provided the Bristol and Exeter Company work those lines efficiently, it is not material whether they employ manual labour, Horses, or Locomotives; and that as they work the Bridgwater Wharf and Sidings with Horses, it would not be reasonable to expect them to employ Locomotives for a similar purpose at Watchet'.

The problem of a wagon shortage also featured in the lengthy report: 'There is ample evidence that the Coal Trade at Watchet has been injured from a want of waggons, but it was admitted on all hands that Bridgwater suffered from the same scarcity.

The best proof of this is the fact that the cargoes have been sent to Exeter via Fremington (near Barnstaple) and the North Devon Railway in consequence of the impossibility of guaranteeing a supply of waggons at Watchet or Bridgwater; and of course all traffic so diverted to Fremington is a loss both to the West Somerset and Bristol and Exeter Companies. The Bristol and Exeter Company are adding to their Stock of waggons, but Watchet will always be at a serious disadvantage as compared with Bridgwater,

Williton station, March 1991. The WSR's preserved No 4561 sits bunker-to-bunker with No 6106, a visitor from Didcot. **PHOTO: PETER HERRING**

Williton station, looking west, September 1964. A Minehead -Taunton DMU pauses at the Up platform. PHOTO: ANDREW MUCKLEY

until private waggons are provided at Watchet, as at Bridgwater...'

Furthermore, it was considered that the WSR was hampered by the lack of a local agent at Watchet, but a solution was suggested: *'.... this deficiency can be best supplied by the appointment of Mr*

Ford, the Harbour Master. He is an intelligent man, well acquainted with the sources of Traffic of the District, and from his position, naturally very anxious to improve the trade of Watchet Harbour. A fixed payment of about £20 a year for his general services as agent, and a commis-

sion of 1d per ton on the increased tonnage from Watchet Station .... (was proposed)'.

Regarding the coal traffic, it appears that the WSR was trying to call the tune. There was, however, a rude awakening in the form of a letter from Mr

Williton station, looking south towards Norton Fitzwarren, 18 July 1970. The 06.20 (SO) Oxford - Minehead train enters the station in the charge of 'Hymek' D7026. The loop on the left shows evidence of recent realignment - otherwise, a train brought right up to the front of the platform would have required passengers to make a giant leap for mankind. The removal of the footbridge is also conspicuous. PHOTO: HUGH BALLANTYNE

Wall of the B&ER to the WSR on 8 March 1870: '*All coal coming from the Watchet Line has to be taken into Taunton in consequence of the West Somerset company not having put in any sidings at Norton Junction. Up to this period, no mileage charge has been made in respect of the Western Traffic, which has to be conveyed from Norton to Taunton and back, a service which entails a serious expense and is entirely borne by this Company.*

I have been desired to give you Notice that on and after the 1st July next, the Mileage referred to will be charged, if the Traffic has so to be conveyed, and the only way of obviating it will be full and sufficient Siding accommodation being made by your Company at Norton Junction'.

Initially, the WSR declined to provide the siding accommodation - later citing a cost of between £700 and £800 for installing a siding - and threatened to take the matter to litigation if the B&ER attempted to enforce the notice. The matter dragged on, Robert Brereton (the B&ER's Chief Engineer) admitting that a siding for 'about 25 trucks .... which would be a double siding or loop' would, in fact, cost between £1,000 to £1,200. A loop was, however, eventually laid.

In 1865 an 8-mile extension from Watchet to Minehead was authorised

in the name of the Minehead Railway, but nothing was done and the company was dissolved in 1870. The WSR was well aware of the usefulness of the proposed extension, the matter having been raised at the Directors' meeting of 15 January 1870: '*This extension would prove a valuable feeder to the West Somerset Line, it would in fact be its "backbone", and it cannot be pressed too strongly on the West Somerset Company the necessity, in their interests, for the completion of this Extension.*

'*It may prove unnecessary to continue the Line on the Broad Gauge system; or it may be found that the original plans may be so modified as to reduce the Cost to an amount that could be readily subscribed in the Locality of the Line*'. The above appears to imply that the WSR had considered taking the Minehead project on board but, if that were indeed the case, it was not to happen.

The Minehead Railway was reconstituted in 1871, and the line was ready for the obligatory Board of Trade inspection on 14 July 1874. The inspector was Colonel Rich, who observed: '*... The permanent way consists of Vignoles pattern rails, that weigh 71lb per lineal yard - it is fished and fixed with facing bolts, to sleepers laid transversely at an average distance of 3ft apart, except the sleepers next to the points of the rails are only 2ft*

apart. The sleepers are 11ft long, 10in x 5in.

'*The following works require to be attended to - a bridge under the railway requires to have the wing walls backed up, as they show signs of hedging. The cutting between Washford and Watchet Station requires to be finished off in places and to have a drain made in the field at the North side to carry off the water and prevent it from soaking through into the Cutting. This Cutting should be watched. A guard rail is required on the 12 chain curve at the West side of the bridge over the Mineral Railway. The locking levers for the facing points on the passenger line are on the ground, but they require to be fixed. The points at Washford require adjusting and the Up Station Signal should be locked with the Siding points*'. That report was not, however, as gloomy as it sounded, the final line declaring that: '*The engineer has promised to have these matters completed at once, and I submit that the Board of Trade may sanction the opening of the Minehead Railway*'.

Like the West Somerset Railway, the Minehead Railway was single track and built to the broad gauge, the Bristol & Exeter Railway working the Taunton - Watchet and Watchet - Minehead sections together as one continuous branch. The Minehead Railway's agreement with

Watchet harbour, cica 1870, Bristol & Exeter broad gauge 4-4-0ST No.64, one of a batch of ten passenger engines built by the Vulcan Foundry in 1867, poses on Watchet turntable. If it is accepted that the 'table was shifted to Minehead when the Watchet - Minehead line opened, this picture must have been taken before 1874. Whatever the case, the date must be before 1876 as, at the start of that year, the B&E was absorbed by the GWR. The engine became GWR No.2074 and survived until the end of the broad gauge in May 1892. PHOTO: VICTOR BONHAM-CARTER COLLECTION

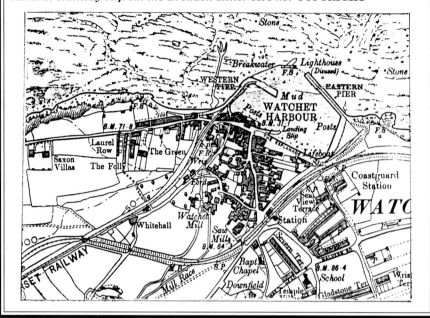

branch trains could, of course, also cross on the double track main line section between Taunton and Norton Fitzwarren. Additional loops were later provided at Bishop's Lydeard, Crowcombe and Blue Anchor, two extra loops being installed in the 1930s. The ruling gradient (and the sharpest on the entire Taunton - Minehead line) was the 1 in 66 between Washford and Blue Anchor.

Whereas Watchet had been a freight-orientated target for the WSR, Minehead was viewed by the Minehead Railway as a potentially lucrative spot for passenger traffic. The small town was a reasonably popular seaside re-

the B&ER had, incidentally, been drawn up on 1st. March 1871.

The Watchet - Minehead line opened on 16 July 1874, and claimed the distinction of being the last new B&ER-worked line to open before that company was gobbled up by the GWR. It had intermediate stations at Washford (19 miles from Taunton station), Blue Anchor (21¼ miles) and Dunster (23 miles). The terminus at Minehead was a little under 25 miles from Taunton. Initially, the branch had crossing places at Williton and Watchet, although

	WATCHET				
	STAFF		RECEIPTS (£)		
Year	No.	Wages	Pass	Goods	Total
1903	7	535	1794	10883	12677
1913	7	488	1995	9210	11205
1923	8	1443	3009	24109	27118
1924	8	1268	2975	23125	26100
1925	8	1619	5294	26326	31620
1926	7	1457	4178	20800	33950
1927	7	1419	3994	28956	32950
1928	7	1485	3276	28630	31906
1929	7	1521	2905	28449	31354
1930	7	1667	2699	26927	29626
1931	6	1567	2719	27725	29994
1932	6	1507	2515	27900	30415
1933	6	1700	2577	27217	29794

Watchet station, looking east towards Norton Fitzwarren, August 1964. Although Watchet was, arguably, the most important stopping place between Taunton and Minehead, the station had only one platform and no passing loop. The footbridge from the station leads to The Cross, more or less at the end of the town's main street (Swain Street). The building on the left is the goods shed. PHOTO: ANDREW MUCKLEY

Watchet, looking west, probably early 1900s. An unidentified outside-framed GWR 0-6-0ST pauses during shunting manoeuvres. The running line of the Taunton - Minehead branch is behind the train and the goods shed (adjacent to the station) is clearly discernible in the distance, while the tracks on the lower level on the extreme right lead to Eastern Pier of Watchet Harbour. The last couple of wagons of the train are alongside the point where the engine shed used to stand - it was on the left-hand side of the running line virtually at the end of the embankment. PHOTO: VICTOR BONHAM-CARTER COLLECTION

Watchet station, looking west, 21 July 1957. The gathering of happy (?) holidaymakers, all clad in coats for their mid-summer outing, seem generally unimpressed by the sight of '43XX' 2-6-0 No 6323 arriving at Watchet with a Minehead - Taunton train. The '43XXs' were not used too frequently on the Minehead branch, due to the problems of turning them at the terminus. PHOTO: HUGH DAVIES COLLECTION

place'. Colonel Horatio Arthur Yorke, incidentally, had been appointed as a Government Inspector of Railways in 1892, and had become Chief Inspector in 1900. He was knighted in 1913 - the year of his retirement - and became a director of the GWR in 1914.

Moving ahead by a few years, the GWR's publicity machine did its bit for Minehead. *Somerset Ways,* published in conjunction with the GWR in 1928, referred to: *'.... the much-maligned little town-ship of Minehead. Much-aligned, because it is so frequently accused of newness, which gives to those who do not know it a very wrong impression'.*

Maxwell Fraser's *Somerset* book for the GWR (1934), stated that: *'Minehead, once rather patronisingly known as a "trippers' paradise", has come into its own since the War. The magnificent hunting, and the neighbouring polo ground on Dunster lawns, gradually attracted wealthy sportsmen who soon fell under the spell of Minehead's very real charm, and so realised that the town was something more than a convenient headquarters for hunting activities....*

'....As the gateway to Exmoor, the only place in the Northern Hemisphere where the ancient sport of Kings - the hunting of the wild red deer - is now obtainable, Minehead attracts sportsmen not only from all parts of the British Isles, but also from America, but whilst the red deer is of course the supreme attraction, Minehead can also afford glorious sport in foxhunting, harehunting and otterhunting, and there are few mornings in the year when the streets are not gay with huntsmen and women riding to the various meets'.

Returning to railway matters of the 1800s, the Bristol & Exeter Railway was absorbed by the GWR on 1 January 1876, and the Taunton - Minehead branch was converted to the standard gauge on 29-30 October 1882. The con-

sort and was also a convenient base for exploring Exmoor; with the increase in the popularity of motor-bus tours in the early 1900s, the town benefited significantly. Indeed, between the mid-1870s and the early 1920s, Minehead's population more than trebled to over 6,000.

In order to cope with the increase in traffic Minehead station was treated to major improvements in 1905, the most conspicuous being the lengthening and widening of the platform. The rebuilt station was inspected for the Board of Trade by Colonel Yorke who, on

22 July 1905, reported on the alterations:

'These comprise the extension of the existing platform, the provision of a new platform line for passenger traffic, alterations in the siding connections, the construction of a new signal box and the re-signalling of the whole place.

'The signal box contains 19 levers in use and 6 spare levers.

'The interlocking being correct and the arrangements satisfactory, I can now recommend the Board of Trade to sanction the use of the new works at this

	WASHFORD				
	STAFF		RECEIPTS (£)		
Year	No.	Wages	Pass	Goods	Total
1903	3	159	1440	2914	4354
1913	3	195	1913	3338	5251
1923	3	542	2330	4169	6499
1924	3	521	2508	3848	6356
1925	3	543	2580	4739	7319
1926	3	472	2434	4394	6828
1927	3	478	2374	4806	7180
1928	3	484	2095	4932	7027
1929	3	476	1856	4608	6464
1930	3	495	1501	4279	5780
1931	3	471	1413	3690	5103
1932	2	452	1367	3635	5002
1933	3	388	1406	3533	4989

MINEHEAD BRANCH.

Single Line worked by Electric Train Staff. The Crossing Stations are Norton Fitzwarren, Bishop's Lydeard, Crowcombe, Williton, Blue Anchor, and Minehead.
The Staff Stations are Norton Fitzwarren, Bishop's Lydeard, Crowcombe, Williton, Watchet, Washford, Blue Anchor, Dunster, and Minehead.
When absolutely necessary two Goods Trains, or a Passenger and a Goods Train may cross at Watchet, Washford or Dunster Stations, on the understanding that the Passenger Train is always kept on the Running Line, and that if the Passenger Train has to stop at either Station it must stop at the Platform.

Down Trains. TAUNTON TO MINEHEAD. Week Days only.

Distance from Taunton (M. C.)	STATIONS.	1 K Goods. arr.	1 K Goods. dep.	2 B Passenger. arr.	2 B Passenger. dep.	3 B Yeovil Passenger. arr.	3 B Yeovil Passenger. dep.	4 B Passenger. arr.	4 B Passenger. dep.	5 B Passenger. arr.	5 B Passenger. dep.	6 K Goods. arr.	6 K Goods. dep.	7 B L'nd'n Excr dep.	8 A Passenger. arr.	8 A Passenger. dep.	9 B Weymouth Passenger. arr.	9 B Weymouth Passenger. dep.	10 A Passenger. arr.	10 A Passenger. dep.	11 B Passenger. arr.	11 B Passenger. dep.	12
—	**Taunton**	A.M.	A.M. 6 25	A.M.	A.M. 8 2	A.M. 9 55	A.M. 10 37	P.M. Q	P.M. 12 17	P.M.	P.M. 1 48	P.M.	P.M. 2 45	P.M. 3 37	P.M.	P.M. 2 40	P.M.	P.M.	P.M.	P.M. 6 22	P.M.	P.M. 7 46	....
2 1	Norton Fitzwarren	R C 8		—	8 8	10 42	10 44	12 22	12 24	—	1 54	2 51	3 0	CS	—	....	5 30	5 45	—	—	7 51	7 53	....
5 9	Bishop's Lydeard	6 43	7 0	—	8 15	10 56	10 58	12 30	12 34	2 0	2 3	3 15	3 35	CS	—	....	5 50	5 52	—	—	8 0	....
8 78	Crowcombe	7 16	7 25	—	8 25	11 1	11 3	—	12 42	2 13	3 50	4 0	CS	—	....	5 58	6 0	—	—	8 9 8 13	....
11 62	Stogumber	7 35	7 43	—	8 31	—	11 9	—	12 48	2 19	4 10	4 20	W	—	....	6 9 6 11	—	—	8 19	....
14 73	Williton	7 53	8 13	8 36 8 39	11 15 11 20	12 53 12 56	2 24 2 26	4 30 4 35 4 30	CS	—	....	6 22 6 26	—	8 24 8 26	8 30	....
16 52	Watchet	8 20 8 53	8 43 8 45	11 24 11 27	1 0 1 3	2 30 2 32	5 35	CS	—	....	6 29 6 32	—	8 30	8 39	....
18 79	Washford	9 1 9 16	8 51 8 53	11 31 11 35	1 9 1 11	2 39	CS	—	....	6 39	—	8 39	....
21 22	Blue Anchor	C S	8 58 9 0	11 39 11 41	1 16 1 24	2 43 2 45	CS	—	....	6 44	—	8 44	....
23 9	Dunster	9 28 9 49	9 2 9 6	11 45 11 50	1 24 1 28	2 49 2 53	xCS	—	....	6 48 6 51	—	8 48 8 51	....
24 64	**Minehead**	9 55	—	9 10	—	11 55	—	1 33	—	2 57	4 29 4 351	5 35	—	....	6 55	—	8 55	....

Q Conveys London Excursion Passengers on Thursdays for Minehead and Lynton. R Calls at Norton Fitzwarren for Traffic for below Watchet only. V Calls where required on Branch for Staff purposes and to set down Passengers from Bristol and beyond and Exeter and beyond; also from the Ilfracombe and Barnstaple Branch. 45 minutes allowed for non-stop, 58 minutes for stoppages. W With London Excursion Passengers, Fridays only. Calls at Bishop's Lydeard, Williton, Watchet, Washford and Dunster, to set down only, if required. To form 11.45 p.m. Y To call at Williton on July 5th and 19th, August 2nd, 16th and 30th, and September 13th and 27th, to pick up Passengers.

Up Trains. MINEHEAD TO TAUNTON. Week Days only.

STATIONS.	1 B Yeovil Passenger. arr.	1 B Yeovil Passenger. dep.	2 B Passenger. MSO arr.	2 B Passenger. MSO dep.	3 B Weymouth Passenger. arr.	3 B Weymouth Passenger. dep.	4 B Yeovil Passenger. arr.	4 B Yeovil Passenger. dep.	5 B Passenger. arr.	5 B Passenger. dep.	6 K Goods. arr.	6 K Goods. dep.	7 B Yeovil Passenger. arr.	7 B Yeovil Passenger. dep.	8 B Yeovil Passenger. arr.	8 B Yeovil Passenger. dep.	9 K Goods. arr.	9 K Goods. dep.	10	11 B Passenger. arr.	11 B Passenger. dep.	12 B Excursion FO arr.	12 B Excursion FO dep.
Minehead	A.M.	A.M. 8 7	A.M.	A.M. 9 26	A.M. 10 46	P.M. 1 5	P.M.	P.M. 2 31	P.M. 3 45	P.M.	P.M. 4 10	P.M.	P.M. 7 28	P.M.	P.M.	....	P.M. 9 20	A.M. 11 45
Dunster	—	8 12	—	9 31	10 50 10 52	1 11 1 18	—	2 36	3 51 4 5	4 14 4 16	—	7 33	....	—	9 24	11 50
Blue Anchor	—	8 17	—	9 36	10 57	1 16 1 18	2 40 2 44	4 11 4 30	4 28 4 21	—	7 38	....	—	9 30	11 55
Washford	—	8 23	—	9 42	11 4	1 23 1 25	—	2 50	4 38 4 56	4 26 4 28	—	7 44	....	—	9 36	12 1
Watchet	8 28	8 30	9 47	9 49	11 9 11 21	1 30 1 32	—	2 56	5 3 5 20	4 33 4 35	7 49 7 51	—	9 41 9 43	12 6	12 5
Williton	8 34 8 37	9 53 9 55	11 16 11 19	1 36 1 38	3 0 3 2	5 25 5 37	4 39 4 41	7 55 7 57	8 0	—	9 47 9 49	12 13	12 15
Stogumber	—	8 45	—	10 5	11 27	—	1 46	—	4 49	8 5	X8 30 8 50	—	9 57	—	12 20
Crowcombe	—	8 53	—	10 11	11 34 11 40	1 54	—	3 16	5 57 X 6 10	4 56 X 4 59	8 12 8 15	CS CR	—	10 5	—	12 25
Bishop's Lydeard	—	9 1	10 10 10 23	11 48	2 1 X 2 4	3 23 X 3 26	8 23	9 12 9 32	—	10 13	—	12 30
Norton Fitzwarren	9 7	9 10	C S	11 54 11 57	R 2 16 2 19	6 52 S T 6 58	5 14 5 16	8 30 8 33	9*44 10 5	—	—	12 46	12 51
Taunton	9 15	9 43	10 55	12 3 12 27	2 24 2 31	3 35 3 35	7 5	5 25	8 39	9 0	10 10	—	.... 10 30	—	12 45

Q Calls for Cattle or ST Goods only. R Five minutes allowed for Signal checks. V Conveys Excursion Passengers for G.C. & L. & N.W., Fridays July 1st to September 16th. W Conveys London Excursion Passengers every Friday, July, August and September, and L. & Y., Birkenhead Line, Midland Railway and Birmingham G.W.R., July 1st to September 16th.

---

version work was undertaken by seven gangs, each of seventy men, who started at daybreak on Sunday 29th and worked so fast that, soon after noon, a 'narrow' gauge special carrying the Divisional Engineer and Traffic Superintendent was able to get through to Minehead.

The two unsung companies, the Minehead Railway and the West Somerset Railway, retained nominally independent status until 1897 and 1922 respectively. Turning once again to the trusty 'Bradshaw's Shareholders' Guide', this time for 1915, the WSR's directors were listed as: The Right Hon. Lord St. Audries of St. Audries, Bridgwater, Messrs. Samuel Fisher and William Henry Fisher of Taunton, Robert Loveband Fulford Esq of 36 Theobald's Road, Gray's Inn, London, and Henry Fuller Acland-Hood, whose address

Washford station, looking east, August 1964. Although public freight facilities were withdrawn from Washford only a month before this picture was taken, the goods shed road (behind the Minehead-bound DMU) appears not to have been over-used for some time. It's a different story nowadays, as the site of Washford's small goods yard is the home for the Somerset & Dorset Trust. The S&D in west Somerset?? The guardians of one of Britain's most charismatic lines failed to secure a site on the S&D itself and, consequently, had to move to 'foreign' parts. PHOTO: ANDREW MUCKLEY

Blue Anchor station, looking east towards Norton Fitzwarren, 9 September 1964, a Taunton - Minehead DMU arriving. As mentioned in the text, the station building at Blue Anchor now houses a superb little museum. PHOTO: ANDREW MUCKLEY

was given as Arthur's Club, St.James's Street, London. (Honest!!!) The name of Acland had been associated with the company since the beginning, the first chairman having been Sir Peregrine Acland while, later, Sir Thomas Acland had made a gift of £500 to the company.

As for services on the branch, the Working Timetable for October 1886 included four passenger trains each way on Mondays - Fridays and five on Saturdays, the average journey times being 75mins from Taunton to Minehead and between 65 and 79mins in the opposite direction. There was also a return freight working each weekday between Taunton and Minehead, and another between Taunton and Watchet.

The WTT noted that the single line was worked by train staff, the staff stations being Norton Fitzwarren, Williton, Watchet and Minehead. The WTT for July to September 1910 listed

Extract from GWR WTT for winter 1947/48.

MAXIMUM LOADS FOR BRANCH FREIGHT TRAINS—continued.

From.	To.	Maximum No. of wagons to be conveyed except for Trains specially provided for in the Service Book or by arrangement.	For Group A Engines.				For Group B Engines.				For Group C Engines.				For Group D Engines.				For Group E Engines.			
			Class 1 Traffic.	Class 2 Traffic.	Class 3 Traffic.	Empties.	Class 1 Traffic.	Class 2 Traffic.	Class 3 Traffic.	Empties.	Class 1 Traffic.	Class 2 Traffic.	Class 3 Traffic.	Empties.	Class 1 Traffic.	Class 2 Traffic.	Class 3 Traffic.	Empties.	Class 1 Traffic.	Class 2 Traffic.	Class 3 Traffic.	Empties.
MINEHEAD.§																						
Norton Fitzw'n	Crowcombe	30	18	22	27	36	21	25	32	42	22	26	33	44	30	35	42	55	—	—	—	—
Crowcombe	Watchet	45	35	42	53	60	35	42	53	70	35	42	53	70	56	61	67	90	—	—	—	—
Watchet	Washford	45	18	22	27	36	21	25	32	42	22	26	33	44	27	33	39	52	—	—	—	—
Washford	Minehead	45	37	44	56	60	37	44	56	74	37	44	56	74	51	56	63	88	—	—	—	—
Minehead	Washford	34	16	19	24	32	18	22	27	36	20	24	30	40	25	30	37	49	—	—	—	—
Washford	Watchet	34	35	42	53	60	35	42	53	70	35	42	53	70	60	66	78	90	—	—	—	—
Watchet	Williton	44	25	30	38	50	29	35	44	58	31	37	47	62	33	40	50	60	—	—	—	—
Williton	Crowcombe	44	18	22	27	36	21	25	30	42	22	26	33	44	33	40	50	60	—	—	—	—
Crowcombe	Norton Fitzw'n	44	35	42	53	60	35	42	53	70	35	42	53	70	65	72	80	90	—	—	—	—

Blue Anchor station, looking west towards Minehead, 18 July 1970. The 1 in 82 climb away from Blue Anchor (heading west) is clearly evident beyond the train (a six-car DMU on the 11.20am Minehead to Taunton service). Three disused camping coaches stand in the siding on the left (behind the level crossing). Blue Anchor was given its first camping coach in the mid-1930s, its second in the late 1950s, and its third (a refugee from the Kingsbridge branch) in 1962. The last summer of camping coach operation on the WR was 1964. PHOTO: HUGH BALLANTYNE

Dunster station, looking east towards Norton Fitzwarren, September 1964. The signal box in the foreground opened in 1934 to replace a box just beyond the far end of the platform. This was part of improvements which included the doubling of the line between Dunster and Minehead (the double-track section commencing on the west side of the level crossing, i.e. behind the photographer). The goods yard - note the superb windows in the office wall - was provided in 1913. PHOTO: ANDREW MUCKLEY

BLUE ANCHOR					
	STAFF		RECEIPTS (£)		
Year	No.	Wages	Pass	Goods	Total
1903	2	98	281	-	281
1913	2	136	469	264	733
1923	3	468	741	493	1234
1924	3	470	735	364	1099
1925	2	459	665	685	1350
1926	2	362	668	361	1029
1927	2	385	678	361	1039
1928	3	487	687	518	1205
1929	3	472	624	592	1216
1930	3	462	615	286	991
1931	3	427	630	574	1204
1932	3	424	676	283	959
1933	2	426	688	363	1051

six 'ordinary' passenger services in the Down direction each weekday, one of which originated at Yeovil and another at Weymouth. There were also three special passenger workings - a Fridays Only excursion from London (calling at five intermediate stations to set down only, if required), a fast train which was allowed only 45 minutes non-stop or 58 minutes if stops were required (setting down only, but with Williton becom-

ing a scheduled pick-up point on seven specified dates), and a Fridays and Saturdays Only working with a similar fast timing. There was also one through goods working, and another which ran only as far as Watchet.

In the Up direction, seven ordinary passenger services were listed, four of which were shown as continuing to Yeovil and another to Weymouth. There was also a Mondays and Saturdays Only passenger working, plus a late evening/early morning Fridays Only train conveying 'London Excursion Passengers every Friday, and L&Y Birkenhead Line, Midland Railway and Birmingham GWR July 1st to September 16th'. The Up goods workings comprised one train from Minehead to Taunton and one from Watchet to Taunton.

Moving ahead to the 1920s, the *GWR Magazine* of December 1923 contained this interesting little report: 'A relic of the past is shortly to be removed from Crowcombe station, on the Minehead branch, this being a length of the bridge rail track which is one of the very few remaining portions of this track which survives in the running lines.

'The Minehead branch .... was first laid on 10in by 7in longitudinal Memel timbers, and kept to gauge with strap bolts through the longitudinals spiked to the transoms. These were replaced with iron tie bolts when the gauge was narrowed in 1882.

'It is only the need for the running of heavier engines on the branch which has

DUNSTER					
	STAFF		RECEIPTS (£)		
Year	No.	Wages	Pass	Goods	Total
1903	3	167	1785	1527	3312
1913	3	205	1340	1842	3182
1923	4	616	2290	3640	5930
1924	4	590	2500	3548	6048
1925	4	594	2452	3784	6236
1926	3	529	2383	3424	5807
1927	3	454	2469	3697	6166
1928	3	450	2339	3728	6067
1929	3	430	2267	3499	5766
1930	3	508	1967	3312	5279
1931	3	458	1931	3415	5346
1932	3	415	1894	2891	4785
1933	3	470	1800	3221	5021

WR Public Timetable, 13 June to 18 September 1955.

Table 82 — TAUNTON, WATCHET and MINEHEAD

Miles		Mondays to Fridays											Fridays only	Saturdays only						
		night	am	am	am	am	pm	am	pm	pm	pm	pm	pm	night	am	am	am	am	am	am P
	61 London (Pad.) 62..dep	11D50	..	5 30	7r30	9R30	..	11R30	1R30	..	3R30	5R30	6r30	11F50	..	..	..	5L30	7r30	9 35
—	**Taunton** .... dep	7a24	9 0	1025	1140	1215	1 40	2p50	4 25	5 49	6 10	8 30	1015	6a55	7 24	8 16	9 0	1020	1140	12p40
2	Norton Fitzwarren	7 30	..	1029	..	1219	..	2 54	4 29	5 53	..	8 34	..	..	7 30	8 21	..	1025	..	..
5	Bishop's Lydeard	7 39	9 10	1036	1150	1225	1 50	3 1	4 35	6 1	6 20	8 41	1025	7 5	7 39	8 29	9 10	1033	1151	....
9	Crowcombe	7 47	9 18	1044	1158	1233	1 58	3 9	4 43	6 10	6 28	8 48	1032	7 13	7 47	8 37	9 19	1042	12 0	..
11¾	Stogumber	7 53	9 23	1050	12 3	1238	2 3	3 15	4 48	6 15	6 33	8 54	....	7 18	7 53	8 43	9 25	1052	12 6	....
15	Williton	8 3	9 33	1059	1211	1249	2 13	3 24	4 57	6 23	6 41	9 2	1045	7 26	8 3	8 53	9 34	11 2	1214	..
16¾	Watchet	8 9	9 39	11 5	1216	1254	2 19	3 29	5 3	6 28	6 46	9 8	1050	7 31	8 9	9 0	9 42	11 9	1219	....
19	Washford	8 16	9 46	1117	1223	1 1	2 26	3 36	5 10	6 35	6 53	9 15	1056	7 38	8 16	9 7	9 49	1116	1226	..
21½	Blue Anchor	8 21	9 51	1122	1230	1 6	2 31	3 41	5 15	6 40	6 58	9 20	11 1	7 45	8 21	9 13	9 55	1121	1233	....
23	Dunster	8 26	9 56	1127	1235	1 11	2 36	3 46	5 20	6 45	7 3	9 25	11 5	7 50	8 26	9 22	10 0	1126	1240	..
24½	**Minehead** .... arr	8 31	10 1	1132	1240	1 16	2 41	3 51	5 25	6 50	7 8	9 30	1110	7 55	8 31	9 27	10 5	1131	1245	1 40

	Saturdays only—*continued*									Sundays												
	am	am P	am	pm	pm	pm	pm	pm		night		am		pm		am		pm		pm		
61 London (Pad.) 62..dep	9 35	1130	1130	12R5	1R35	3R30	5R30	6r30	..	11s50	..	..	..	..	..	11R0	..	1R30	..	3R30	..	..
Taunton .... dep	1p 5	2p20	2p55	3 25	4 45	6 15	8 30	1015	....	8a50	....	1150	....	1 15	....	2 40	....	4 45	....	6 55	....	....
Norton Fitzwarren	1 10	..	2 59	..	4 49	6 19	8 34	..	..	8 54	..	..	..	1 19	..	2 45	..	4 49	..	6 59	..	..
Bishop's Lydeard	1 20	....	3 6	....	4 57	6 26	8 41	1025	....	9 0	....	12 0	....	1 26	....	2 53	....	4 55	....	7 5	....	....
Crowcombe	1 29	..	3 15	3 48	5 6	6 34	8 48	1032	..	9 8	..	12 8	..	1 35	..	3 1	..	5 3	..	7 13	..	..
Stogumber	1 35	....	3 21	....	5 12	6 40	8 54	....	....	9 14	....	1214	....	1 42	....	3 7	....	5 9	....	7 20	....	....
Williton	1 44	2 55	3 32	4 5	5 21	6 48	9 2	1045	..	9 23	..	1223	..	1 52	..	3 16	..	5 18	..	7 29	..	..
Watchet	1 51	....	3 39	4 11	5 26	6 55	9 8	1050	....	9 28	....	1228	....	1 58	....	3 21	....	5 23	....	7 34	....	....
Washford	2 2	..	3 46	4 19	5 34	7 2	9 15	1056	..	9 35	..	1235	..	2 5	..	3 36	..	5 35	..	7 40	..	..
Blue Anchor	2 7	....	3 53	4 32	5 40	7 7	9 20	11 1	....	9 40	....	1240	....	2 10	....	3 41	....	5 40	....	7 46	....	....
Dunster	2 14	..	4 0	4 38	5 47	7 14	9 25	11 5	..	9 45	..	1245	..	2 15	..	3 46	..	5 45	..	7 51	..	..
Minehead .... arr	2 20	3 20	4 5	4 43	5 52	7 20	9 30	1110	....	9 50	....	1250	....	2 20	....	3 51	....	5 50	....	7 56	....	....

Miles		Mondays to Fridays											Fridays only	Saturdays only						
		am	am	am	pm	pm	pm	pm	pm	pm	pm	pm	pm	am	am	am	am	am P	am	pm W
—	**Minehead** .. .. .. dep	7 35	9 5	10 50	12 20	1 45	2 55	4 30	5 10	6 10	7 30	8 5	9 50	7 35	8 25	9 5	10 5	1040	1155	1220
1¾	Dunster	7 40	9 9	10 54	12 24	1 49	2 59	4 34	5 14	6 14	7 34	8 9	9 55	7 40	8 29	9 10	10 11	..	12 0	1225
3¼	Blue Anchor	7 45	9 14	10 59	12 29	1 54	3 4	4 39	5 21	6 19	7 39	8 14	9 59	7 45	8 34	9 16	10 17	..	12 6	1232
5¾	Washford	7 50	9 20	11 5	12 35	2 0	3 10	4 45	5 27	6 25	7 45	8 20	10 5	7 50	8 40	9 22	10 24	....	1214	1238
8	Watchet	7 56	9 26	11 12	12 41	2 6	3 16	4 51	5 33	6 33	7 51	8 26	1011	7 56	8 46	9 29	10 31	..	1225	1244
9¾	Williton	8 3	9 32	11 19	12 47	2 12	3 21	4 57	5 39	6 41	7 58	8 33	1018	8 3	8 52	9 36	10 38	....	1232	1250
13	Stogumber	8 10	9 40	11 26	12 55	2 19	3 29	5 4	5 46	6 49	8 5	8 40	..	8 10	..	9 43	10 45	..	1239	1258
15¾	Crowcombe	8 17	9 47	11 32	1 1	2 25	3 35	5 10	5 52	6 56	8 12	8 48	1033	8 17	....	9 50	10 54	....	1246	1 5
19¾	Bishop's Lydeard	8 24	9 54	11 40	1 9	2 33	3 43	5 18	6 0	7 4	8 20	8 57	1041	8 24	..	9 59	11 3	..	1254	1 13
22¾	Norton Fitzwarren	8 30	10 0	11 46	....	2 39	....	5 24	6 6	7 10	8 26	9 3	....	8 30	....	10 6	11 10	....	....	....
24½	**Taunton** .. .. .. arr	8 35	10 5	11 51	1 23	2 44	3 56	5 35	6 11	7 15	8 31	9 8	1055	8 35	9 20	10 11	11 17	1140	1 10	1 26
167½	61 London (Pad.) 62.. arr	12R10	1R30	2R50	5R35	6G15	7K10	....	9R 0	....	....	....	5a 0	....	12R15	1U20	2 40	2 40	....	5R15

	Saturdays only—*continued*									Sundays												
	pm	pm P	pm	pm	pm	pm	pm	pm	pm		am		pm		pm		pm		pm		pm		
Minehead .. .. .. dep	1 35	2 15	3 0	4 20	5 5	5 50	6 35	7 50	9 50	..	1020	..	1 40	..	3 10	..	5 10	..	6 30	..	8 25	..	..
Dunster	1 39	....	3 4	4 24	5 10	5 54	6 40	7 54	9 54	....	1024	....	1 44	....	3 14	....	5 14	....	6 34	....	8 29	....	....
Blue Anchor	1 45	..	3 12	4 30	5 16	6 0	6 46	7 59	9 59	..	1029	..	1 49	..	3 19	..	5 19	..	6 39	..	8 34	..	..
Washford	1 51	....	3 18	4 37	5 22	6 6	6 52	8 5	10 5	....	1035	....	1 55	....	3 25	....	5 25	....	6 45	....	8 40	....	....
Watchet	1 57	..	3 24	4 44	5 33	6 12	7 2	8 11	1011	..	1041	..	2 5	..	3 31	..	5 31	..	6 51	..	8 46	..	..
Williton	2 4	....	3 31	4 50	5 40	6 19	7 9	8 17	1018	....	1048	....	2 12	....	3 38	....	5 38	....	6 58	....	8 53	....	....
Stogumber	2 11	..	3 40	4 58	5 48	6 26	7 16	8 25	..	..	1055	..	2 19	..	3 45	..	5 45	..	7 5	..	9 0	..	..
Crowcombe	2 19	....	3 48	5 7	5 55	6 35	7 23	8 32	1033	....	11 2	....	2 26	....	3 52	....	5 52	....	7 14	....	9 7	....	....
Bishop's Lydeard	2 27	..	3 57	5 17	6 3	6 43	7 31	8 40	1041	..	1110	..	2 34	..	4 0	..	6 0	..	7 23	..	9 15	..	..
Norton Fitzwarren	2 33	....	4 4	5 24	6 9	6 49	7 37	8 46	....	....	....	....	2 40	....	4 6	....	6 6	....	7 29	....	9 21	....	....
Taunton .. .. .. arr	2 42	3 20	4 15	5 30	6 15	6 55	7 42	8 55	1055	..	1120	..	2 45	..	4 11	..	6 11	..	7 35	..	9 26	..	..
61 London (Pad.) 62.. arr	6 25	6 25	....	....	9R 5	....	....	....	5a0	....	3R45	....	....	....	7R20	....	9R30	....	....	....	3a25	....	....

a am
D Sunday to Thursday nights
F Friday nights only
G Change at Bristol (T.M.); limited accommodation Bristol to London. Refreshment Car provided
K Refreshment Car Train. On Fridays passengers can arr 6 50 pm without Refreshment Car
L Dep 7 0 am on Saturdays 25th June to 20th August inclusive; Refreshment Car to Taunton

P Through train between London and Minehead
p pm
R Refreshment Car between Paddington and Taunton
r Refreshment Car Paddington to Bristol
s Saturday nights
U Through train Minehead to London 2nd July to 10th September inclusive only. Arr 1 35 pm on 18th, 25th June and 17th September with Refreshment Car from Taunton

W Through carriages Minehead to Birmingham (S.H.) and Wolverhampton (L.L.)

A Road Motor Service is operated by the Western National Omnibus Company between Minehead, Porlock Village and Lynmouth

For OTHER TRAINS between Taunton and Norton Fitzwarren, see Tables 81 and 84

even now rendered necessary the relaying of this portion of the line, for the road, apart from the timbers, is still good for several years for the small engines which at present work the branch. The original weight of this pattern of bridge rail was about 68lb per yard'.

Crowcombe was also mentioned in the GWR Traffic Committee minutes of 9 October 1924: *'Extension of siding accommodation £460. The cost being borne as follows: By the Company £80; By the Trader interested £380, to be rebated to him on the basis of 5% on the receipts from his traffic'.*

During the general strike of 1926, one of the volunteer guards on the Minehead branch was - according to an oft-repeated story - a former station master at Paddington. After the strike came a long period of depression which, combined with the increasing competition from road transport, did the nation's branch and rural railways no good at all. In many spheres, however, the GWR realistically accepted that it couldn't win all of the battles against the internal-combustion engined rival and, instead, made use of the opposition's main weapon.

One of the GWR's tactics was the introduction in 1927 of 'Land Cruises', *'...a combination of first-class rail travel and de luxe motor coach touring through different areas on the Company's system, embracing places and districts famous for their historic associations and scenic beauty.*

'In each case the fares charged are inclusive of rail and road transport, first-class hotel accommodation with table d'hote meals, gratuities to hotel servants, and admission fees to places of interest visited during the tour'.

So what has this to do with Minehead? The 'Land Cruise' programme for 1933 (and possibly for previous years also) included the West Somerset and North Devon coasts, one of the overnight stopping places being at Minehead. That section of the tour was, however, undertaken by road. For the record, the passengers were taken from Paddington to Bath by train on the Monday, spent the following four days in their 'de luxe motor coach', and rejoined a train (the 12 noon 'Torbay Express') at Torquay the following Saturday. The fare in 1933 was 12 guineas.

The 'Land Cruises' were clearly targeted at those whose bank balances were little affected by the economic climate, but the general passenger traffic - especially during the summer seasons - on the Minehead branch remained very healthy during the mid-1920s, although there was the inevitable decline during the recession-hit late-1920s and early 1930s. Despite the nation-wide financial gloom of the early 1930s, the branch was earmarked for a degree of investment, although it is probable that the extensive 'Loan Act' modernisation to the railway system in the Taunton area helped to trigger thoughts of improving the Minehead branch. One aspect of the Taunton improvements was the quadrupling of the main Bristol - Exeter line through Taunton, Norton Fitzwarren station (where the Minehead branch diverged from the main line) subsequently being rebuilt with two island platforms. The proposed improvements to the Minehead branch were featured in the June 1933 issue of the *GWR Magazine: 'A scheme of improvements is to be carried out by the Great Western Railway Company on the Minehead branch. These will enable accelerations of five to fifteen minutes to be effected in the journey times of trains between Paddington and Minehead, and also considerably improve the working of trains by the elimination of delays formerly experienced during the summer months. 'At present, on the 22 miles of line - which is a single one - between Norton Fitzwarren and Minehead, there are four crossing places where trains may pass each other, viz., at Bishops Lydeard, Crowcombe, Williton, and Blue Anchor.*

'The projected scheme provides for the construction of two further crossing places, one at Leigh Bridge (between Crowcombe and Williton) and the other at Kentsford (between Williton and Blue Anchor). These will have the effect of dividing the two longest sections on the branch.

'The crossing loops, which will be 750 feet in length, are to be constructed to enable trains to pass through them at a speed of 40 miles per hour, apparatus being provided on the engines and at the

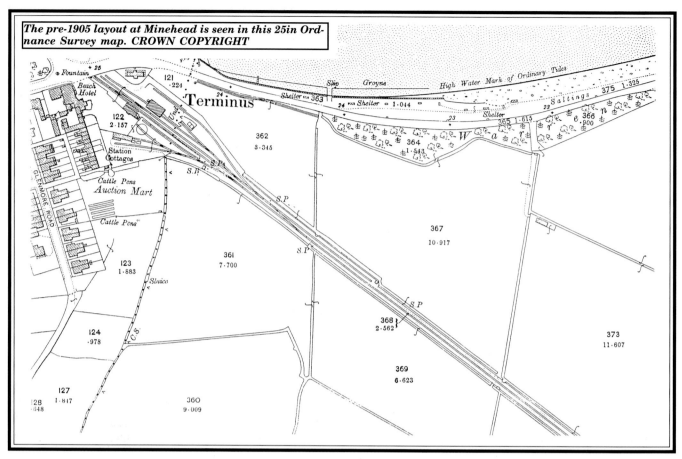

loops to enable the single line tokens to be exchanged automatically. A new signal box will be constructed at each new loop, and at Minehead station the existing platform covering is to be extended by 200 feet.

'The improvements, which will be brought into use in time for the opening of the summer service in July next year, have been made necessary by the increasing popularity of Minehead as a holiday resort'.

Perhaps surprisingly, that article did not include details of proposed doubling, the section from just beyond the station at Dunster to Minehead (1¾ miles) being doubled in March 1934, and the Norton Fitzwarren - Bishop's Lydeard section (3¼ miles) in June 1936. Also omitted were references to the lengthening of the platforms at Crowcombe, Stogumber, Watchet, Washford and Dunster, the work being undertaken in the spring/early summer of 1934.

The heralded acceleration of services on the Minehead branch was, however, not particularly startling. The following table opposite shows journey times (in minutes) at selected dates during a 33-year period, the figures in brackets referring to the total number of services (first figure weekdays, second figure Saturdays). N.B: 7/1922: one additional train each way Fridays only. 5/1943: Saturdays Only trains for

Table 1		7/1922	3/1940	6/1943	11/1946	10/1947	6/1955
Taunton - Minehead		70-75 (7/7)	63-70 (7/7)	66-73 (7/10)	63-70 (11/11)	65-75 (8/8)	55-75 (11/15)
Minehead - Taunton		66-77 (7/7)	63-69 (7/7)	63-69 (7/9)	63-70 (11/11)	63-72 (8/8)	60-75 (11/16)

Table 2	1/1908	2/1908	1/1909	2/1909	1/1910	2/1910	1/1911	2/1911	1/1912	2/1912
Receipts (£)	3527	5528	3706	5692	3802	5768	3752	5635	3497	5731
Expenses (£)	3249	3179	3080	3316	3124	3734	3310	3333	3063	3346
Balance (£)	278	2331	626	2376	678	2034	442	2203	434	2385

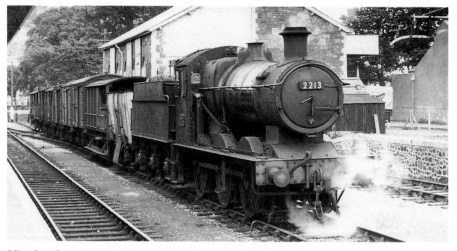

Minehead station, 26 June 1958. The '2251' 0-6-0s had a long supremacy on the Minehead line, but it was usually Taunton- or Minehead-based ones which were used. Here, however, No 2213 displays the shedplate of St.Philip's Marsh in Bristol while shunting at Minehead. PHOTO: J. DAVENPORT

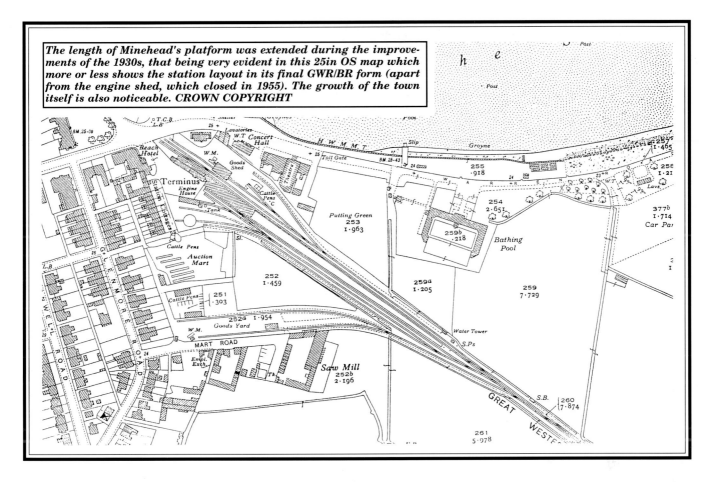

late June to early Sept only, two each way having through carriages to and from Paddington; also three Sunday services each way. 10/1947: one additional train each way on Mondays (a.m.) and Fridays (p.m.). 6/1955: one additional train each way on Fridays; Saturday services included through train each way Paddington - Minehead, and one with through carriages to Birmingham and Wolverhampton; also six trains each way on Sundays. Sunday services were, incidentally, usually a feature of only the summer timetables.

Turning once again to the beloved WTTs - in this case, the one for 6 October 1947 to 30 May 1948 - in addition to the passenger services, two daily freight workings were shown each way between Taunton and Minehead, with one each way between Taunton and Watchet. The working instructions stated that all 'Blue' engines except 28XX and 78XX types were per-

mitted, as well as all 'Yellow' types. The 78XXs were, however, permitted between Taunton and Bishop's Lydeard, as were 49XX 'Halls'. The only two prohibitions noted were that no engines were to pass the stopboards at the harbour yard coal siding at Watchet, or at Watchet Paper Mill. The loading limits for passenger trains were 360 tons for 2-6-0s and heavier 2-6-2Ts

MINEHEAD					
	STAFF		RECEIPTS (£)		
Year	No.	Wages	Pass	Goods	Total
1903	11	635	9898	7986	17853
1913	14	965	12947	11807	24754
1923	19	3011	21477	20237	41714
1924	19	3028	18805	19509	38314
1925	19	3391	20954	19550	40504
1926	19	2805	20814	19350	40164
1927	19	2962	20289	19904	10193
1928	19	3240	19808	20639	10447
1929	19	3394	18570	18292	36862
1930	20	3603	17520	19224	36744
1931	20	3401	15789	16208	31997
1932	20	3417	14714	14658	29372
1933	19	3453	14512	13750	28262

Minehead station forecourt, late 1800s. PHOTO: JOHN L SMITH

19

PASSENGER RATED TRAFFIC : MINEHEAD						
	TICKETS		RECEIPTS (£)			
Year	Ord	Season	Pass	Pcls	Misc	Total
1903	35070	n/a	6140	1664	2094	9898
1913	48578	n/a	8770	2211	1966	12947
1923	45906	87	15549	1495	4433	21477
1924	42708	77	15096	1486	2223	18805
1925	43985	82	16124	1487	3343	20954
1926	38610	76	15484	2931	2399	20814
1927	38987	81	14575	3195	2519	20289
1928	32801	62	14046	3258	2504	19808
1929	29978	48	13027	3158	2385	18570
1930	28159	21	12185	3215	2120	17520
1931	26144	28	11118	3050	1621	15789
1932	25230	33	10430	3109	1175	14714
1933	25307	33	9731	3453	1328	14512

Minehead station, 1960s. A break in the early morning cleaning-up, presumably.
PHOTO: JOHN L SMITH

Minehead, 26 June 1958. It was necessary to use extension bars when turning 2-6-0s and 4-4-0s on Minehead's 45ft 'table, and so such engines were not used on the Minehead line with any real regularity. PHOTO: J. DAVENPORT

the first train of the day from Minehead was timed to depart before the arrival in the town of the first train from Taunton, an engine was outstationed at the small timber-built engine shed adjacent to Minehead station. It has been suggested elsewhere that the shed building and the 37ft 8in turntable had previously stood at Watchet in the days when the branch had terminated there, but were moved to Minehead when the extension opened in 1874. However, the pre-opening Board of Trade inspection commented on the presence of a turntable at Minehead, and it must be asked if the 'table at Watchet would really have been taken away while that latter point was still the terminus of the line.Whatever the case, Minehead eventually finished up with a 45ft 'table which, in later years at least, posed problems with the turning of 2-6-0s and 4-4-0s.

As for the shed building, this scribe has been unable to unearth official documentation which either confirms or disproves the 'relocation' suggestion, but photographs of Watchet shed show a structure with curved-topped doors whereas the shed at Minehead

(albeit with a 310 ton limit for Up trains between Minehead and Washford), 260 tons for the lighter (44XX, 45XX and 55XX) 2-6-2Ts, most 0-6-0PTs and the 3306-3455 series of 4-4-0s, 250 tons for other 4-4-0s and 2251 class 0-6-0s, and 200 tons for 14XX class 0-4-2Ts.

Going back to the turn of the century, the usual form of motive power was either 'Metro' 2-4-0Ts or 0-6-0STs. As

Minehead, 1901. For many years, the 'Metro' 2-4-0Ts were the GWR's archetypal branch and suburban locomotives. They were introduced in 1869 for working on the Metropolitan Railway (for which they were fitted with condensing apparatus), but construction continued until 1899. The last survivors were withdrawn in 1949. No 1453 was built in January 1882 and lasted until July 1933.

Minehead station, early 1950s. '2251' 0-6-0 No 2213 waits at Minehead. Is that routinely-acquired grime, or has it been parked under a tree? PHOTO: JOHN L SMITH

had unmistakably straight-topped doors. That said, it is perfectly feasible that Watchet and Minehead sheds were one and the same building, and that the doors were modified at some stage.

Looking at the latter-day motive power situation a little more closely, the Swindon register for 1909 reveals that all Minehead shed's residents that year were 'Metros' - No 1455 until 27 March, then No 626 until 23 April, followed by No 463 which remained for the rest of the year. The 1920 register also shows a 'Metro' monopoly at Minehead - No 3588 until 23 May, then No 975 until 20 June, followed by No 3588 again (20 June to 7 November) and No 461 (10 October until 5 December); No 985 then took over until 2 January 1921, when it was replaced by No 456. Unfortunately, the reason for an allocation of two engines (Nos 3588 and 461) between 10 October and 7 November remains a mystery. Dual allocations featured on several other occasions over the years but, perhaps surprisingly, not usually during the summer months when peak traffic could be anticipated.

At the start of 1928, 45XX class 2-6-2T No 4525 was listed as living at Minehead, the Prairies having taken over from the 'Metros' during the previous year. Random 'first week of January' allocations contained in the Swindon registers (and provided by Mr Bill Peto of the GWR Society) included No 4591 (1930), No 5542 (1934), Nos 5503/

37 (1937), No 5571 (1942), and No 5542 (1943).

Although the allocation lists showed a Prairie monopoly from the late 1920s to the early 1940s, 4-4-0 tender engines had been introduced on the line in the 1920s. The 4300 class 2-6-0s were also occasionally used on the Minehead line, but they didn't fit readily on to Minehead's 45ft turntable (extension

bars being required) and so their use was never as frequent as on the nearby Taunton - Barnstaple line.

The 1942 allocation lists show that 2251 0-6-0 and No 2230 had a spell at Minehead between February and June 1942. Classmate No 2268 was recorded as taking over from 2-6-2T No 5503 in May 1943, and from then on it was an 0-6-0 monopoly at Minehead with, on

Minehead station, 21 July 1957. '43XX' No 6323, wearing what looks like the 83A shedplate of Newton Abbot, runs round its train. PHOTO: HUGH DAVIES COLLECTION

Minehead station, late 1950s. '2251' No 2277 (minus a shedplate) shunts a rake of assorted wagons at Minehead. PHOTO: R.S. CARPENTER.

occasions, two of the class allocated there simultaneously. Random 'first week of January' lists include No 2213 (1948) and No 2211 (1953), the latter spending much of that year at Minehead. By the mid-1950s, however, 57XX 0-6-0PTs were the most usual steeds on passenger duties, although the 2251s were still regularly used on freight turns.

Minehead shed, which had usually employed two sets of men, closed in November 1956. In subsequent years, the usual practice was for the first train on the line each day to be an engine and van from Taunton to Minehead which provided the engine for the first train (a passenger service) ex-Minehead. At the end of the working day, the engine off the last Taunton - Minehead train returned to Taunton with a van.

It is quite possible that, ever since its inception, BR had been looking for a WTT revision which would permit the closure of Minehead shed. The WTT inherited by BR in January 1948 had shown that the first train on the line was the 5.45am goods ex-Taunton arriving at Minehead at 7.15am, thus (in theory at least) providing the engine for the first ex-Minehead train of the day - the 7.35am passenger service. However, the stumbling block came at the end of the day, the last working on the branch (Fridays excepted) being the 9.5pm Taunton - Minehead passenger which, of course, left the engine at Minehead.

In the late 1950s, Standard 'Class 3' 2-6-2Ts appeared on the Minehead line, the February 1959 issue of *Trains Illustrated* including the observation that: *'...the Class "3" 2-6-2Ts recently transferred to Bath Road shed, Bristol, have visited Taunton; from November 11-13 (1958) one of them was noted on a diagram covering the 7.48am Bristol - Taunton, the 10.25am Taunton - Minehead and the 12.20pm back'.* During the early 1960s, the large 61XX 2-6-2Ts were seen on the line, some-

times double-heading with 'Type 2' diesels.

This writer is indebted to Mr Eric Youldon of Exeter who has provided report of his trip on the line on Tuesday 26 June 1960. Mr Youldon travelled behind 2-6-2T No 5563, and observed 0-6-0PT No 9757 being passed at Williton on the Down journey, while 0-6-0 No 2277 (with a goods train) and No 5503 were passed at Watchet and Williton respectively on the return trip. A lovely selection of classic Swin-

Minehead station, 21 July 1957. '51XX' class 2-6-2T No 4157 prepares to leave for Taunton. PHOTO: HUGH DAVIES COLLECTION

don engineering. Interestingly, Mr Youldon noted that, in common with many other summer-time journeys on the line, his Minehead-bound train collected a significant number of passengers en route, so that there were far more alighting at Minehead than had embarked at Taunton. This was somewhat unusual for a country branch line.

The Taunton - Minehead branch escaped the Beeching cuts, but one economy effected in 1964 was the withdrawal of public freight facilities. The branch's last freight spur - to the paper mill at Watchet - was removed in 1967. Somewhat ironically, Watchet Harbour saw an increase in trade during the mid-1960s, but there were, by then, no railway connections left to assist in the transportation of goods.

Minehead and the West Somerset coast remained very popular with holidaymakers, the establishment of a holiday camp at Minehead providing a further boost for the town's fortunes but, inevitably, an increasing number of the holidaymakers made their journeys by road. Passenger services were retained on the Minehead branch only until Saturday 2 January 1971, diesel multiple units having taken over most of the local passenger workings as from 10 September 1962. Diesel locomotives — mainly the 'Hymeks' and the North British 'Type 2s' - had taken over the through holiday workings in the very early 1960s, but as the decade progressed, the operation of longer-dis-

tance summer Saturday trains declined. By the final summer (1970), there had been two Paddington - Minehead workings, one Minehead - Paddington service and a Minehead - Oxford train, but these had been provided by InterCity DMUs.

Just four months after BR's closure of the Minehead branch, a preservation group was formed under the familiar title of the West Somerset Railway. After negotiations, Somerset County Council bought the branch, complete with track still in position, and leased the whole lot to the preservation company. The Minehead - Blue Anchor section reopened in March 1976 (*do* have a look at the fascinating little museum at Blue Anchor station) and, in June 1979, the line was reopened through to Bishop's Lydeard. With a twenty mile run, the 'new' WSR boasts the distinction of having the longest preserved line in Britain. For some time, the question of the WSR running through to Taunton frequently caused near apoplexy among the folks at BR, but negotiations eventually resulted in an agreement for occasional through running via the Taunton Cider Company's yard. The first through train ran on 16 June 1990.

As a different option in the preservation field, Messrs. Butlins - the proprietors of the holiday camp at Minehead - had two conspicuous residents for several years. They were ex-LMSR 4-6-2 No 6229 DUCHESS OF HAMILTON and former LBSCR 'Terrier'

0-6-0T No.32678, both of which had been restored for static display.

The 'Duchess' had made its way to Minehead on 29 April 1964, hauled by 0-6-0PT No 9647, arriving at 10am after a journey which, due to severe speed restrictions, had taken three hours from Taunton. On its arrival at Minehead, the Pacific was propelled on to the turntable, and was turned half a circle on to a special track which had been laid across the site of the old engine shed and on to the trailer of a 50-ton Pickford's low-loader. The loading and transfer to the holiday camp was completed by 7 May. Ironically, that usage of the Minehead turntable was, it is believed, the very last. The 'Duchess' remained at Minehead until 10 March 1975, when it was taken by low-loader to the station, re-railed, and three days later hauled to Taunton by Type 2 diesel No 25029. From Taunton, it was taken to BREL Swindon for renovation before being transported to the National Railway Museum at York.

The journey of the 'Terrier' to Minehead in July 1964 was a little less exciting - it was conveyed on a well wagon. It left the holiday camp in April 1975, though it moved only as far as Williton on the recently-preserved West Somerset line. As a final word on the preservation aspect, Washford station is now the headquarters of the Somerset & Dorset Museum Trust, the Trust's preserved S&D 2-8-0 (BR No 53808) being a regular performer on the West Somerset line.

Minehead station, September 1964. Public goods facilities were withdrawn from Minehead in July 1964 - a couple of months before this picture was taken - but a BR lorry is nevertheless up to something on the far side of the shed. A Taunton-bound DMU waits. PHOTO: ANDREW MUCKLEY

Norton Fitzwarren station, looking west, believed to be late 1930s. Norton Fitzwarren was the point where the Minehead and Barnstaple branches diverged from the main Taunton - Exeter line, and the route of the Minehead branch is visible behind the second carriage. The 'Bulldog' 4-4-0 arrives off the Barnstaple branch, which is just out of view to the left. Although undated, this picture was clearly taken after 1931, when the re-building of Norton Fitzwarren station with two island platforms was completed. PHOTO: JOHN SMITH

RAILWAY HOTEL

TAUNTON to BARNSTAPLE

The Devon & Somerset Railway, which was backed largely by local landowners, had to undergo a bout of corporate fisticuffs with the London & South Western Railway when promoting its broad gauge line between Taunton and Barnstaple. The LSWR's opposition was largely due to its recent acquisition of the lease on the Exeter - Barnstaple line, but the South Western's monopoly of North Devon was not to last long, as the Devon & Somerset Railway received assent on 29 July 1864.

Matters initially looked rosy for the D&SR, for on the day of its incorporation, a line between Barnstaple and the holiday resort of Ilfracombe was also authorised by Parliament, with the D&SR empowered to become joint owners with the L&SWR and to provide mixed gauge rails. However, the D&SR soon found that it could not come up with its share of the capital for the line, and was formally released from its obligation in 1867. As things turned out, the L&SWR eventually let its own interest in the project lapse, and Ilfracombe did not get a railway until 1874.

The D&SR's inability to raise half the cost of the Ilfracombe extension was a reflection of the company's poor financial position. The 1869 issue of 'Bradshaw's Shareholders' Guide' stated that the works were in abeyance, and added that: *'It was reported in August (1868) that a scheme of arrangement had been filed in the Court of Chancery, as the only means of relieving the company from its diffi-* *culties and of enabling it to prosecute the works to completion of the undertaking'.*

Work eventually resumed, and the seven or more miles between Watchet Junction (two miles west of Taunton near the site where Norton Fitzwarren station was later built) and Wiveliscombe was finally opened on 8 June 1871. The remaining 35 1/4 miles between

Barstaple branch sations : Livestock traffic (Vans forwarded & received)													
Station	1903	1913	1923	1924	1925	1926	1927	1928	1929	1930	1931	1932	1933	1913=100
Milverton	140	104	94	117	160	141	105	146	147	103	98	66	53	38
Wivelscombe	302	346	356	433	378	483	473	486	495	531	462	440	398	132
Venn Cross	50	54	64	61	114	94	125	128	142	90	82	52	43	86
Morebath	52	87	77	85	75	82	49	83	80	93	91	90	48	92
Dulverton	430	378	351	366	431	487	413	461	400	428	406	395	275	64
East Anstey	60	209	320	287	287	246	301	269	280	294	282	226	194	93*
B. Nympton	260	202	195	268	260	239	268	283	266	286	289	217	160	61
South Molton	579	601	386	549	539	519	524	531	531	569	507	320	210	36
Filleigh	127	186	103	117	86	109	147	135	128	182	214	92	66	52
Swinbridge	12	97	17	19	15	16	14	9	29	14	12	4	1	8
Barnstaple	576	688	622	642	659	618	643	685	722	752	570	282	166	29
Totals	2588	2952	2585	2944	3004	3034	3062	3216	3220	3342	3013	2184	1614	62

* 1914 = 100

Taunton station, 23 July 1962. '43XX' 2-6-0 No 7333 rests at Taunton with the empty stock from a train from Barnstaple Junction. PHOTO: ROGER PALMER

| DEVON and SOMERSET.—Bristol and Exeter. |

Paddington Station,	1&2	1,2,3	1&2	1,2,x	1,2	1,2	Up.	1,2,3	1&2	1,2	1&2	1,2	1,2	1&2
LONDON 2 ....dep	...	...	6 45	1145	1030	1550	Barnstaple......dep	7 40	9c15	1030	2 0	3c30	5 25	9 0
BRISTOL 3 .... ,,	6 15	8 10	1030	2 26	3 15	6 0	Swimbridge......	7 53	...	1043	2 13	...	5 35	9 10
EXETER 6 .... ,,	6 0	8 50	1115	1225	4 45	6 0	Castle Hill ..	8 5	...	1055	2 25	...	5 44	9 19
Taunton ....dep	7 50	1045	1 0	3 30	5 35	8 15	South Molton [Molland	8 18	9c47	11 8	2 38	3c57	5 56	9 31
Norton Fitzwarren ..	7 59	1052	1 6	3 31	5 41	8 24	Bishop's Nympton and	8 33	...	1123	2 53	...	6 9	...
Milverton............	8 14	11 5	1 17	3 47	5 52	8 39	East Anstey	8 49	...	1139	3 9	...	6 22	...
Wiveliscombe	8 26	1115	1 28	3 58	6 3	8 51	Dulverton ......[ton]	9 6	1014	1121	3 21	4 27	6 36	...
Venn Cross..... [ton]	8 41	1129	1 42	...	6 17	9 6	Morebath (for Bamp-	9 14	...	12 1	3 31	...	6 44	...
Morebath (for Bamp-	8 54	1140	1 51	...	6 26	9 19	Venn Cross	9 24	...	1212	3 42	...	6 55	...
Dulverton............	9 6	1151	2 2	4 27	6 36	9 31	Wiveliscombe	9 37	1038	1226	3 58	4 53	7 8	...
East Anstey [Molland	9 20	12 5	2 14	...	6 48	9 45	Milverton............	9 45	...	1236	4 8	...	7 16	...
Bishop's Nympton and	9 34	1219	2 26	...	7 0	9 59	Norton Fitzwarren ..	9 58	1052	1249	4 22	5 9	7 29	...
South Molton	9 47	1232	2 35	4 55	7 15	1012	Taunton 6, 3 ....arr	10 5	1055	1255	4 32	5 15	7 35	...
Castle Hill	9 57	1242	2 48	...	7 23	1022	BRISTOL 6 ....arr	1140	12 4	2 35	6 30	6 45	9 50	...
Swimbridge	10 7	1252	2 58	...	7 33	1032	EXETER 3 ....,,	1230	1 30	3 10	6 45	6 43	9 51	...
Barnstaple 37 ....arr	1020	1 5	3 10	5 15	7 45	1045	LONDON 7 .... ,,	2 45	2 45	6 0	1030	1020	3 55	...

Wiveliscombe and Barnstaple were not opened until 1 November 1873 (to goods on 11 November). As early as 1865, the D&SR had entered into a working agreement with the Bristol & Exeter Railway under which the gross receipts were to be split 50-50, but even when the B&ER was absorbed by the GWR in 1876, the D&SR continued to maintain a separate corporate existence. It was not until 1901 that the GWR finally took over the D&SR, by which time the latter had notched up over £500,000 in arrears of debenture interest. The unsung little company had not exactly been the proverbial gold mine for shareholders.

The intermediate stations between Taunton and Barnstaple were at Milverton (61/4 miles from Taunton station), Wiveliscombe(91/2 miles), Venn Cross (141/2 miles), Morebath (173/4 miles), Dulverton (211/4 miles), East Anstey (25 miles), Molland (30 miles), South Molton(343/4 miles), Castle Hill (371/2 miles) and Swimbridge (41 miles). Molland was renamed Bishop's Nympton & Molland on I March 1876, and Castle Hill was retitled Filleigh on 1 January 1881, an additional stopping place being provided at Norton Fitzwarren (where the branch diverged from the main Taunton - Exeter line two miles west of Taunton) on 1 August 1873.

As mentioned elsewhere in this book, Norton Fitzwarren station was rebuilt in the early 1930s as part and parcel of the extensive quadrupling works in the Taunton area, the 'new' twin-island platform station at Norton Fitzwarren opening on 2 December 1931, a couple of months or so before the completion of the quadrupling works. In February 1937 the junction layout at Norton Fitzwarren was modified so that the Barnstaple line connected directly with the main line, instead of diverging from the Minehead branch as had previ-

Norton Fitzwarren, 5 September 1950. 2-6-0 No 6377 pulls away from Norton Fitzwarren with a Barnstaple train. The tracks diverging to the right (seen in front of the engine) are, however, the start of the Minehead branch. PHOTO: R.S. CARPENTER

| | MILVERTON | | | | |
| | STAFF | | RECEIPTS (£) | | |
Year	No.	Wages	Pass	Goods	Total
1903	3	202	1302	1743	3045
1913	3	235	1323	1986	3309
1923	4	587	2230	3742	5972
1924	4	519	2200	3212	5412
1925	4	611	1985	3857	5842
1926	4	572	1847	4082	5929
1927	4	588	1561	4623	6184
1928	4	582	1443	3690	5133
1929	4	586	1375	3641	5016
1930	4	608	1143	3335	4478
1931	4	603	973	2481	3454
1932	3	582	915	2172	3078
1933	3	507	853	2214	3067

Norton Fitzwarren, looking south-west, 5 September 1950. The double-track main line to Exeter disappears in the distance, the start of the Barnstaple branch (the two parallel tracks) running on the right-hand side of the Exeter line. The lines diverging behind the Railway Hotel (on the right) are those of the Minehead branch. Until 1937, the Barnstaple lines diverged from the Minehead lines, and not from the main line as illustrated here. PHOTO: R.S. CARPENTER

ously been the case. That work was undertaken in conjunction with the doubling of the Norton Fitzwarren-Milverton section of the Barnstaple line - also completed in February 1937.

On the Barnstaple line, there had initially been plans for stations at Landkey and Leary, but neither was built. Nevertheless, two new halts were eventually added. The first was Morebath Junction halt (19¼ miles from Taunton), which opened on 1 December 1928 at the point where the Exe Valley line joined the Barnstaple line to the east of Dulverton station. The second was Yeo Mill halt between East Anstey and Bishop's Nympton (26½ miles), which opened on 27 June 1932.

The branch terminus at Barnstaple (over 44 miles from Taunton) had only a single platform, albeit with a bay along part of the rear face, but its goods facilities were reasonably extensive and the original timber-built goods shed was eventually replaced by a substantial stone-built five-bay shed. There was also a twin-road engine shed in wood, and it is believed that its original turntable had previously been used at Wiveliscombe during the 2½ years when the latter had been the temporary terminus of the line. For much of its life, the terminus at Barnstaple had only a single-word title, the suffix 'Victoria Road' not being appended until 26 September 1949. As could be expected for a route across West Somer-

set and North Devon, the Taunton - Barnstaple line abounded in heavy gradients, 1 in 60 being encountered with uncomfortable frequency. The line incorporated two handsome viaducts, both of wrought iron lattice girders resting on stone piers - Castle Hill Viaduct near Filleigh (232yd long and 94ft high), and Tone Viaduct to the east of Venn Cross (162yd long and 101ft high). There were also three tunnels - Bathealton (440yd), Venn Cross (246yd) and Castle Hill (317yd).

It should not go unmentioned that there was once a narrow gauge horse-worked tramway which connected with an exchange siding on the Barnstaple line near South Molton. The tramway was constructed in 1874 to serve Florence Mine, where modest quantities of iron ore were extracted, and in 1877 a branch was laid to Croborn Iron Mine. The mines and the tramway were abandoned in 1894, although during each of the World Wars attempts were made to reopen them. Interestingly, WTTs for the Barnstaple line for the 1880s and 1890s listed 'Florence Siding', just under 34 miles from Norton Fitzwarren Junction.

The Taunton - Barnstaple line was converted to the standard gauge in 1881. The last broad gauge train left Barnstaple on the evening of Saturday 14 May, and although a huge army of platelayers was brought in from other districts, it was Wednesday 18th before the standard gauge service could commence. Even then, only two passenger trains each way and one goods train ran on the 18th, full services not being resumed until the following day.

It was anticipated that the line would attract some traffic to and from the beauty spots of Lynton and Lynmouth which, at the time, had no rail connection. It appears that a Mr Bush proposed to operate a horse-bus service between South Molton station and Lynton (presumably with the aid of a railway company subsidy), the following estimate being supplied to the GWR:

1 Brake	£150
1 Van in reserve	£70
3 Setts 4-horse harnesses	£90
Clothing and Stable Utensils	£30
20 Horses at £50	£1000
TOTAL	£1340

'Coach to start from Lynton say at 8.30am to meet 11 o'clock Train at South Molton to arrive in London at 6pm.
'Leaving South Molton at 3pm after arrival of 9am Train from London.
'There would be 4 horses at Lynton stables; at South Molton 4 horses; at Friendship Inn 8 horses; at Parracombe 2 horses.

Milverton station, looking west towards Barnstaple, circa 1920s. The Up platform with its small shelter was added circa 1880, the Norton Fitzwarren - Milverton section being doubled throughout by February 1937. The dead-end road running from the Up platform into the mid-distance was a relief siding. PHOTO: JOHN L SMITH

Milverton station, looking west, September 1964. Public goods facilities were withdrawn from the station at the end of September 1963, and it is evident that little time had been wasted in removing the sidings from the small yard behind the Down platform. PHOTO: ANDREW MUCKLEY

Extra in reserve: 2 horses.

TOTAL:

20 horses @ 17/-	*£17.0s.0d*
2 Coachmen @ 25/-	*£2.10s.0d*
1 Guard @ 20/-	*£1.0s.0d*
6 Stablehands @ 20/-	*£6.0s.0d*
1 ditto Parracombe	*£1.0s.0d*

Rent of Stabling horses:
5 South Molton
8 Friendship Inn
2 Parracombe

5 Lynton	*£2.10s.0d*
Turnpike 12/- per day	*£3.12s.0d*

TOTAL :	*£33.12s.0d*

The response came from the 'Coaching Department, Barnstaple Station' on 3 January 1880:

'*Assuming that you work a single Coach and start from Lynton in the morning, changing halfway and leaving South Molton in the afternoon, you would not keep horses at the South Molton end.*

'*To work the Coach well and be prepared for any mishaps, you would require 12 horses, 4 for the journey each way working half the distances, and two kept midway for helping up hills, also a spare at midway and spare at Lynton. My idea of the cost of working, leaving aside your capital outlay, would be as under:*

12 Horses, weeks keep:	*£10.4s.0d*
Coachman:	*£1.5s.0d*
Guard:	
(this man to attend to Horses at South Molton in day while waiting train):	*£1.0s.0d*
2 Stablemen (one at Lynton and one at midway):	*£2.0s.0d*

In addition to these charges you have Stable rent as you may arrange, and Tolls. I have assumed keep of Horses on about quantities we keep our own Ilfracombe Coaching Horses'.

For those avidly waiting to hear the conclusion of that gripping little episode, a disappointment awaits. Sadly,

Milverton station, looking east towards Norton Fitzwarren, 28 September 1963. Mogul No 7332 leaves Milverton with the 5.55pm Taunton - Barnstaple train. No 7332 was one of the '93XXs' which, between 1956 and 1959, had been modified to fill the gaps left by withdrawn '43XX' 2-6-0s. The modifications resulted in a reduction in weight (to 'Blue' status), and the rebuilds were therefore permitted to work the Barnstaple line, from which they had hitherto been barred. PHOTO: HUGH BALLANTYNE

	WIVELSCOMBE				
	STAFF		RECEIPTS (£)		
Year	No.	Wages	Pass	Goods	Total
1903	6	296	2700	4918	7618
1913	5	317	2815	5088	7903
1923	6	876	3889	8414	12303
1924	6	856	3442	8648	12090
1925	6	875	3266	9076	12342
1926	6	807	3086	8599	11685
1927	6	827	3403	8391	11794
1928	6	733	3134	9204	12338
1929	6	830	2857	8840	11679
1930	6	840	2649	8212	10861
1931	7	884	2635	8271	10636
1932	7	943	2289	7030	9319
1933	7	1000	2114	7739	9843

Above:- Milverton station, looking west, possibly late 1940s/early 1950s. A 'Dean Goods' 0-6-0 shunts wagons. PHOTO: JOHN L SMITH

Below:- Wiveliscombe station, looking towards Barnstaple, 21 July 1964. Although services on the Taunton - Barnstaple line still had a couple of years left when this picture was taken, it seems that the station staff at Wiveliscombe had already started to ignore the cosmetic appearance of the Up platform. No.7337 is in charge of the 10.40 Barnstaple - Taunton working. PHOTO: ROGER PALMER

later documents do not seem to have survived.

Apart from Lynton and Lynmouth, much of the Taunton - Barnstaple line's catchment area was a potential tourist attraction. One of the likely spots to entice visitors was the small town of Dulverton, although it might be argued that the GWR - sponsored book *Somerset Ways* of 1928 did not exactly smack of over-sell: '*Dulverton, a low-built, sleepy township, claims to be the capital of Moor-land.* [but so did a few other towns and villages, according to the very same book] *Truly it is a valley of delight where this jumble of red homes and grey lies half hidden in the woods. Dulverton is right on the edge of the moor, so it has less the essential moorland character than Exford has, which is why Exford in its turn claims to be capital of Exmoor.'* Maxwell Fraser's '*Somerset Ways'*, written for the GWR in 1934, performed a somewhat more poetic piece of PR for Dulverton: '*.... the adorably impetuous little river Barle rushes hurriedly through Dulverton .... Dulverton is one of those places which have no relics of their history, and yet suggests an atmosphere of the past more successfully than many a town filled with medieval buildings'.*

Returning to mainstream railway matters, one of the early narrow gauge WTTs for the Taunton - Barnstaple line

This extract from the Working Timetable for the winter of 1947/48 shows the loading limits for freight trains on the Taunton - Barnstaple line.

MAXIMUM LOADS FOR BRANCH FREIGHT TRAINS.

SECTION		WORKING LOADS. Maximum No. of wagons to be conveyed except for Trains specially provided for in the Service Book or by arrangement.	MAXIMUM ENGINE LOADS.																		
			For Group A Engines.				For Group B Engines.				For Group C Engines.				For Group D Engines.				For Group E Engines.			
			Class of Traffic.				Class of Traffic.				Class of Traffic.				Class of Traffic.				Class of Traffic.			
From.	To.		1	2	3	E'ties.	1	2	3	E'ties.	1	2	3	E'ties.	1	2	3	E'ties.	1	2	3	E'ties.
BARNSTAPLE‡																						
Norton Fitzw'n	Milverton	V 32	15	18	23	30	17	20	26	34	19	23	29	38	25	30	38	50	—	—	—	—
Milverton	Wiveliscombe	V 32	15	18	23	30	16	19	24	32	20	26	34	44	23	28	35	46	—	—	—	—
Wiveliscombe	East Anstey	V 32	14	17	21	28	15	18	23	30	17	20	26	34	21	26	32	42	—	—	—	—
East Anstey	South Molton	16	16	19	24	32	18	22	27	36	22	26	33	44	26	31	39	52	—	—	—	—
South Molton	Barnstaple	—	14	17	21	28	18	18	22	30	17	20	26	34	24	28	39	52	—	—	—	—
Barnstaple	Barnstaple Jct.	V 32	14	17	21	28	15	18	23	30	17	20	26	34	21	26	32	42	—	—	—	—
Barnstaple Jct.	Barnstaple	V 32	18	22	27	36	19	23	29	38	21	25	32	42	28	34	42	56	—	—	—	—
Barnstaple	Wiveliscombe	V 32*	14	17	21	28	15	18	23	30	17	20	26	34	21	26	32	42	—	—	—	—
Wiveliscombe	Norton Fitzw'n	V 32	18	22	27	36	19	23	30	38	21	25	32	42	26	31	39	52	—	—	—	—

V—4.5 a.m. Taunton to Barnstaple, 35 wagons Class 3 traffic. (*42 from Dulverton to Taunton on 8.15 p.m. ex Barnstaple.)

VENN CROSS					
	STAFF		RECEIPTS (£)		
Year	No.	Wages	Pass	Goods	Total
1903	2	96	494	1019	1513
1913	3	158	465	785	1250
1923	3	486	609	1142	1751
1924	3	487	537	1453	1990
1925	3	505	453	1442	1895
1926	3	507	440	1480	1920
1927	3	508	468	1721	2189
1928	3	501	338	1780	2118
1929	3	515	378	1595	1973
1930	3	517	370	1952	2322
1931	3	517	306	1629	1935
1932	3	505	273	1430	1703
1933	3	525	282	1295	1577

Left:- Wivelisombe station, looking towards Barnstaple, 23 July 1962. '43XX' No 6340 waits with the 14.24 Barnstaple Junction - Taunton train. Note the Whitaker apparatus on the tender. PHOTO: ROGER PALMER

- for October 1886 - listed five passenger services each way on weekdays, the average journey time for the 44½ mile trip being a little under two hours. The WTT also featured two goods workings each way on weekdays (although the early morning Taunton - Barnstaple train was not scheduled to run on Mondays) and a Down working on Sundays. It was noted that the single line was worked by train staff, the staff 'stations' being Norton Fitzwarren, Milverton, Wiveliscombe, Morebath, Morebath Junction, Dulverton, East Anstey and Bishops Nympton.

Of the staff 'stations' mentioned above, Morebath Junction was not, at the time, actually a station. It was merely the point one and a half miles west of Morebath where the delightful Exe Valley branch from Exeter via Tiverton joined the Taunton - Barnstaple line. However, as mentioned earlier, Morebath Junction halt was provided near the junction in 1928. The northern section of the Exe Valley line opened on 1 August 1884, the trains starting

Venn Cross station, looking east, 23 June 1965. The North British 'D63XX' diesel-hydraulics took over many West Country duties previously entrusted to 2-6-2Ts. Here, No D6337 enters Venn Cross from the direction of Norton Fitzwarren; Venn Cross tunnel is in the background. PHOTO: MICHAEL MENSING

Table 84 **TAUNTON, DULVERTON, BARNSTAPLE and ILFRACOMBE (Week Days only)**

Miles		Mondays to Fridays								Saturdays only											
		night	am	am	am	pm	pm	pm	pm	night T	night D	night T	am T	am	am T	pm	am K	pm W	pm T	pm	pm
	61 London (Pad.) 62..dep	11d50	5 30	9R30	11R30	1R30	..	3R30	5R30	11F50	11F50	11F50	..	5H30	9 35	..	1130	12R5	1R35	3R30	5R30
—	**Taunton** .... dep	8a 3	10 13	12p15	2p44	4 35	5 45	6 17	8 25	5a20	6a20	7a15	8 30	1025	12p50	1 48	2 25	3 35	4 35	6 17	8 35
2	Norton Fitzwarren	..	10 19	12 19	..	4 39	5 49	..	..	..	..	7 19	8 34	1029	..	1 54	..	..	..	6 22	..
6¼	Milverton	8 17	10 28	12 27	2 57	4 47	5 57	6 31	8 37	....	....	7 28	8 43	1037	1 3	2 2	....	....	4 47	6 30	8 47
9¼	Wiveliscombe	8 25	10 35	12 34	3 4	4 54	6 4	6 38	8 44	5 40	6 40	7 36	8 51	1046	1 12	2 10	2 44	..	4 54	6 37	8 54
14½	Venn Cross	8 36	10 46	12 45	3 15	5 5	6 15	6 49	8 55	....	....	7 47	9 4	1058	1 24	2 22	....	....	5 5	6 48	9 5
17¼	Morebath	8 42	10 52	12 51	3 21	5 10	6 21	6 55	9 1	..	..	7 55	9 10	11 4	1 30	2 28	..	..	5 10	6 54	9 11
19¼	Morebath Junction Halt ..	8 47	10 57	12 56	3 29	5 16	6 26	....	9 6	....	....	....	9 15	1110	....	2 33	....	....	5 16	6 59	9 16
21	Dulverton	8 53	11 3	1 2	3 35	5 22	6 30	7 5	9 12	6 5	7 5	8 5	9 21	1118	1 43	2 39	3 15	4 23	5 25	7 5	9 24
24¾	East Anstey	9 3	11 13	1 11	3 44	5 31	....	7 14	9 21	....	....	8 14	9 30	1128	1 54	2 48	....	....	5 34	7 14	9 35
26½	Yeo Mill Halt	9 8	11 18	1 15	3 49	5 36	..	7 18	9 26	..	..	..	9 35	1133	1 59	..	..	..	5 39	7 18	9 40
30	Bishop's Nympton and	9 14	11 24	1 21	3 55	5 42	....	7 27	9 34	....	7 25	8 26	9 41	1139	2 5	2 58	....	....	5 47	7 26	9 46
34¼	South Molton ...[Molland	9 23	11 33	1 29	4 3	5 50	..	7 34	9 43	6 30	7 34	8 35	9 49	1147	2 13	3 7	3 43	4 50	5 55	7 34	9 54
37½	Filleigh	9 32	11 42	1 38	4 12	6 0	....	7 43	9 52	....	....	8 44	9 58	1156	2 22	3 17	....	....	6 5	7 43	10 3
40¾	Swimbridge	9 39	11 49	1 45	4 20	6 7	..	7 50	9 59	..	..	8 51	10 5	12 5	2 30	3 24	..	..	6 14	7 50	1010
44¾	**Barnstaple** arr	9 46	11 56	1 52	4 28	6 14	....	7 57	10 6	6 52	7 55	8 58	1012	1212	2 38	3 31	4 10	5 11	6 22	7 57	1017
	Victoria Road.. dep	9 51	12 4	2 0	4 34	6 19	..	8 4	..	7 10	8 4	9 4	1030	1220	2 54	3 46	4 19	5 15	6 36	8 4	..
45½	**Barnstaple Junction** arr	9 57	12 10	2 5	4 40	6 25	....	8 10	....	7 16	8 10	9 10	1035	1226	3 0	3 50	4 25	5 22	6 42	8 15	....
60¾	**Ilfracombe** .. .. „	10 52	1 48	3 40	5 56	7 17	..	9 4	..	8 12	9 5	9 58	1122	2A 5	3 56	..	5 10	6 16	7 37	9 4	..

Miles		Mondays to Fridays									Saturdays only												
		am	am	am	pm	pm	pm	pm	pm	pm	am	am	am M	am N	am D	am P	noon	pm	pm	pm	pm B	pm B	pm W
—	**Ilfracombe** .. .. dep	..	..	8 55	1220	..	3 0	.	.	5 45	..	6 42	8 25	9 25	1012	1055	12 0	..	2 55	..	5 10	6 30	8 0
15	**Barnstaple Junction** „	....	....	10 0	1 10	2 25	3 58	....	....	6 40	....	7 45	9 10	1016	11 3	1142	1242	2 5	3 55	4 55	5 53	7 15	8 43
16	**Barnstaple** arr	..	..	10 5	1 16	2 30	4 3	.	.	6 45	..	7 50	9 17	1023	1110	1150	1248	2 10	4 0	5 0	6 0	7 22	8 50
	Victoria Road.. dep	6 55	8 20	1010	1 20	2 35	4 12	525	...	6 54	6 55	7 56	9 25	1027	1120	1155	1253	2 20	4 10	5 14	6 5	7 25	8 54
20	Swimbridge	7 2	8 27	1018	1 29	..	4 20	532	.	7 2	7 2	8 3	..	1035	1130	..	1 1	2 30	4 18	..	6 14	7 34	..
23½	Filleigh	7 9	8 34	1025	1 38	....	4 28	541	...	7 9	7 9	8 10	....	1043	1138	....	1 8	....	4 26	....	6 22	7 43	....
26½	South Molton ...[Molland	7 17	8 42	1033	1 47	2 55	4 37	552	.	7 17	7 17	8 18	9 50	1051	1150	1218	1 16	2 46	4 34	5 38	6 31	7 52	9 16
30¾	Bishop's Nympton and	7 25	8 50	1041	1 55	....	4 46	6 3	...	7 25	7 25	8 26	....	1059	1158	....	1 24	2 57	4 44	5 46	6 39	8 1	....
34¼	Yeo Mill Halt	7 32	8 57	1048	2 2	..	4 53	.	.	7 32	7 32	8 33	..	11 6	12 5	..	1 30	..	4 51	..	6 46	8 8	..
36	East Anstey	7 37	9 3	1053	2 7	....	4 58	617	...	7 37	7 37	8 38	....	1111	1211	....	1 35	....	4 57	....	6 51	8 13	....
39¾	Dulverton	7 45	9 15	11 2	2 15	3 20	5 9	630	7 5	7 45	7 45	8 47	1016	1120	1220	1245	1 43	3 17	5 8	6 8	7 3	8 26	9 44
41¼	Morebath Junction Halt ..	7 51	9 20	11 8	2 22	....	5 14	...	7 9	7 51	7 51	8 52	....	1126	1225	....	1 49	....	5 14	....	7 9	8 31	....
43	Morebath	7 54	9 24	1110	2 25	..	5 18	641	712	7 55	7 54	8 55	..	1130	1229	..	1 53	..	5 18	..	7 12	8 35	..
46¼	Venn Cross	8 2	9 32	1119	2 33	....	5 26	655	720	8 3	8 2	9 3	....	1138	1237	....	2 1	....	5 26	....	7 20	8 43	....
51½	Wiveliscombe	8 11	9 41	1129	2 42	3 45	5 36	7 8	732	8 12	8 11	9 12	1045	1148	1247	1 12	2 10	3 42	5 36	6 36	7 32	8 55	1010
54½	Milverton	8 17	9 47	1135	2 47	....	5 42	715	738	8 18	8 17	9 18	....	1154	1253	....	2 16	....	5 42	....	7 38	9 2	....
58¾	Norton Fitzwarren	8 25	9 55	..	..	..	5 50	.	746	8 26	8 25	9 26	..	12 2	1 1	..	2 24	..	5 50	..	7 46	9 10	..
60¾	**Taunton** .... arr	8 30	10 1	1148	3 0	4 3	5 55	728	751	8 31	8 30	9 31	11 3	1210	1 6	1 30	2 31	3 57	5 55	6 55	7 51	9 18	1030
203¾	61 London (Pad.) 62.. arr	12R10	1R30	2R50	6G15	7R10	9R 0	.	.	..	12R15	1V35	2 40	..	..	5R15	6 25	7U15	9R 5	..	..	..	5a 0

A On Saturdays 2nd July to 13th August arr 1 27 pm
a am
B Through Train Ilfracombe to Taunton
D Through Train between Taunton and Ilfracombe. Runs 16th July to 27th August inclusive only
d Sunday to Thursday nights
F Friday nights only
G Change at Bristol (T.M.); limited accommodation from Bristol. Refreshment Car available
H On Saturdays from 25th June to 20th August inclusive dep 7 0 am. Refreshment Car to Taunton.
K Through Carriages London to Ilfracombe
M Through Train Ilfracombe to Bristol (T.M.). Commencing 2nd July extended to Manchester (Ex.), arr 6 48 pm (Table 168)
N Through Train Ilfracombe to Cardiff (Tables 61 and 104)
P Through Carriages Ilfracombe to Wolverhampton (L.L.) (Tables 61 and 169)
p pm
R Refreshment Car between Paddington and Taunton
T Through Train Taunton to Ilfracombe
U Refreshment Car available 25th June to 20th August inclusive only
V Refreshment Car Train. From 2nd July to 10th September passengers can arr 1 20 pm without Refreshment Car
W Through Train between Taunton and Ilfracombe. Runs 18th June to 10th September inclusive only

A Road Motor Service is operated by the Southern National Omnibus Company between Barnstaple Junction and Chelfham Cross, Bratton Fleming, Blackmoor Gate, Parracombe Woody Bay Cross and Lynton.

For OTHER TRAINS between Taunton and Norton Fitzwarren, see Tables 81 and 82—Morebath Junction Halt and Dulverton, Table 87.

WR public timetable, 13 June to 18 September 1955. As explained in the text, don't be fooled by the apparent abundance of through workings to and from Ilfracombe. They were not always what they seemed.

supply of sprags in his Van for this purpose. Great care must be taken to remove the sprag from the wheel before starting. (Sprag: 'a bar inserted to stop a wheel; a device to prevent a vehicle from running backwards') *The speed of all Trains passing over the Castle Hill Viaduct, near Filleigh, and the Tone Viaduct, near Venn Cross, must not exceed 15 miles per hour'.*

Despite its failure to come up with the money for the proposed joint line between Barnstaple and Ilfracombe, the D&SR still viewed access to Ilfracombe as extremely beneficial. In its early years, the D&SR had pressed the L&SWR for a joint station at Barnstaple (which would have permitted through traffic between Taunton and Ilfracombe), but the powers at Waterloo had, in view of the D&SR's precarious financial state, not been over-enthusiastic.

The scheme for a joint line to Ilfracombe faded into obscurity, but the L&SWR soon put its corporate weight behind the allegedly independent Barnstaple & Ilfracombe Railway, which proposed a line between the towns of its title. The line opened on 20 July 1874 but, frustratingly for the D&SR and Bristol & Exeter (and, later, the GWR), there was no rail connection between the D&SR terminus and the L&SWR stations. That matter was, however, eventually resolved.

In 1884 the GWR proposed a line of its own between Barnstaple and Ilfracombe. It was little more than a scare tactic, but it worked. The L&SWR subsequently agreed that, if the Bill were dropped, through carriages from the GWR line could indeed be taken on to

and terminating at Dulverton station. Until 1890 Exe Valley services used the Down platform at Dulverton, but the station was then remodelled with the Down platform becoming an island, Exe Valley trains subsequently using the rear of the platform.

Referring once again to the 1886 WTT for the Taunton - Barnstaple line, the working instructions stated that: *'No Train or Engine must run past any facing point on the Devon and Somerset Railway at a greater speed than 10 miles per hour. When running down the inclines the speed must not exceed 30 miles per hour with Passenger Trains and 15 miles per hour with Goods Trains. The Guard in charge of every Train when he may have occasion to shunt vehicles on or near an incline is strictly ordered not to allow the Engine to be uncoupled until he has securely put on the brake and safely spragged the last vehicle, and he must not commence his journey without he has a*

Venn Cross station, looking west towards Barnstaple, 21 July 1964. Venn Cross station actually straddled the Devon/Somerset border, which ran across the station immediately behind the signal box (on the Down platform). The start of the 1 in 60 drop from the west end of the station is very evident. Taunton-based 2-6-0 No 7337 is seen with the 10.40 Barnstaple Junction - Taunton working. PHOTO: ROGER PALMER

Morebath station, looking east towards Norton Fitzwarren, September 1964. The station was still operational when this picture was taken, although the loop (which had been laid in 1876 and extended in 1937) has clearly gone. Just evident on the right of the picture is part of the wooden platform extension, tacked on in 1937. The brick structure on the right is the partly-demolished signalbox. A sorry state of affairs indeed. PHOTO: ANDREW MUCKLEY

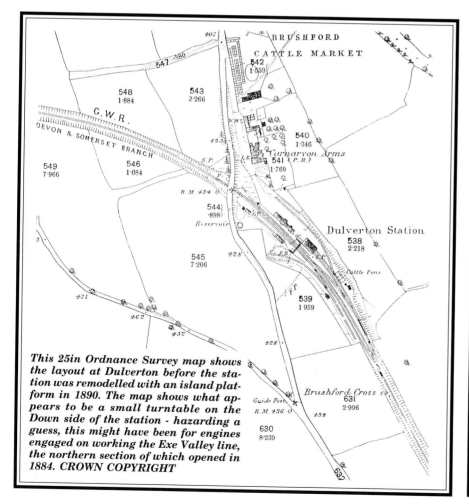

This 25in Ordnance Survey map shows the layout at Dulverton before the station was remodelled with an island platform in 1890. The map shows what appears to be a small turntable on the Down side of the station - hazarding a guess, this might have been for engines engaged on working the Exe Valley line, the northern section of which opened in 1884. CROWN COPYRIGHT

Ilfracombe by the L&SWR. This necessitated the construction of a connecting spur, some one and a quarter miles in length, between the GWR branch terminus and the L&SWR line (to the south of Barnstaple Junction). It opened on 1 June 1887. As if to pave the way for the through carriages to Ilfracombe, the GWR had already inaugurated a horse-bus service between the Barnstaple terminus and Ilfracombe. This had not amused the L&SWR, but it had at least got some of the inter-company hostilities out of the way prior to the commencement of the through carriage workings.

A further improvement was made on 1

	MOREBATH				
	STAFF		RECEIPTS (£)		
Year	No.	Wages	Pass	Goods	Total
1903	2	129	507	671	1178
1913	3	191	634	890	1524
1923	3	460	987	1340	2327
1924	3	451	990	1345	2335
1925	3	496	917	1565	2482
1926	3	433	864	1424	2288
1927	3	450	888	1385	2273
1928	3	476	842	1511	2353
1929	3	479	719	1478	2197
1930	3	483	874	2067	2941
1931	3	414	830	1655	2485
1932	3	372	546	1357	1903
1933	3	409	455	942	1397

Dulverton station, looking east towards Norton Fitzwarren, 29 February 1964. The disappearance of the smokebox number-plate from forlorn '43XX' No 5336 might suggest that withdrawal was imminent - the evil day, however, was seven months away, in September. The carriages of the 1.15pm Taunton - Barnstaple Junction train appear to have been treated to a little more spit and polish than the locomotive. PHOTO: HUGH BALLANTYNE

Dulverton station, looking west towards Barnstaple, 23 July 1962. 2-6-0 No 6340 arrives at Dulverton with the four-coach 14.24 Barnstaple - Taunton train. An Exe Valley auto-train stands on the far side of the island platform. PHOTO: ROGER PALMER

Dulverton station, looking east, August 1964. The Exe Valley side of the island platform at Dulverton has fallen into disuse after the withdrawal of services from that route on 7 October 1963. The removal of Dulverton's goods yard is underway, although public goods facilities had been withdrawn from the station only a month before this picture was taken. Dulverton station was actually in the village of Brushford, some two miles from Dulverton itself, but it was nevertheless the second busiest intermediate station on the Taunton - Barnstaple line. Its hey-day was, of course, a little before this picture was taken. PHOTO: ANDREW MUCKLEY

Dulverton station, looking east, September 1964. A two-car DMU waits to leave for Barnstaple. The tidy appearance of the station is in marked contrast to that of some others on the line during the same year. PHOTO: ANDREW MUCKLEY

East Anstey station, looking east towards Norton Fitzwarren, September 1964. The station was, at 800ft above sea level, the highest point on the Taunton - Barnstaple line. The loop was added in 1876 and was extended in 1910, while a relief siding (forming an extension of the loop - behind the photographer) was laid in 1937. PHOTO: ANDREW MUCKLEY

July 1905 with the opening of Barnstaple East Loop, which permitted through running between Taunton (GWR) and Barnstaple Junction (L&SWR) without the need for a reversal at the GWR terminus in Barnstaple. In practice, however, from the mid-1920s the loop was open only during the summer season, but after the cessation of summer services in September 1939 Barnstaple East Loop remained closed

for over twenty years. Nevertheless, an additional bonus from the outset was that, as the turntable at Barnstaple terminus could accommodate only tank engines, the triangle formed by the new

East Loop was useful for turning tender engines.

The WTT for the summer of 1910 listed eight passenger trains each way on weekdays, all but one of which in each

DULVERTON					
	STAFF		RECEIPTS (£)		
Year	No.	Wages	Pass	Goods	Total
1903	15	455	5428	6197	11625
1913	8	484	4680	6552	11232
1923	10	1510	6725	11260	17985
1924	10	1468	6977	10797	17774
1925	10	1443	7161	11930	19091
1926	10	1247	7104	10871	17975
1927	10	1300	7138	10906	18044
1928	10	1366	7155	10631	17786
1929	10	1428	7134	12595	19729
1930	12	1619	6792	10165	16975
1931	12	1806	5847	8920	14767
1932	12	1692	5537	8348	13885
1933	12	1827	5059	7543	12602

East Anstey station, looking east, 21 July 1964. The station was deprived of its public goods facilities in December 1963, hence the shed's apparent state of disuse. The anonymous Mogul at the head of the 13.15 Taunton - Barnstaple Junction train is No 7306. PHOTO: ROGER PALMER

Yeo Mill halt, September 1964. Opened in June 1932, the halt could accommodate only a single carriage. Colonel Stephens might well have fancied this one, had he still been around. PHOTO: ANDREW MUCKLEY

BISHOP'S NYMPTON					
	STAFF		RECEIPTS (£)		
Year	No.	Wages	Pass	Goods	Total
1903	3	163	1024	1378	2402
1913	3	200	994	1468	2462
1923	3	445	1376	2635	4011
1924	3	481	1290	3103	4393
1925	3	498	1164	2957	4121
1926	3	503	1121	2656	3777
1927	3	479	1126	2828	3954
1928	3	475	995	2971	3966
1929	3	465	972	2868	3840
1930	3	481	856	2781	3637
1931	3	459	773	2773	3546
1932	3	442	776	2264	3040
1933	3	444	719	1902	2621

Bishops Nympton & Molland, looking east towards Norton Fitzwarren, 23 July 1962. The station became a passing place in 1876, and had its platforms extended during the general branch improvements of 1937. Taunton's 2-6-0 No 6372 waits with the 11.15 Taunton - Barnstaple Junction train. PHOTO: ROGER PALMER

EAST ANSTEY					
	STAFF		RECEIPTS (£)		
Year	No.	Wages	Pass	Goods	Total
1903	7	173	1564	1372	2936
1913	3	198	1134	1620	2754
1923	4	492	1164	2893	4057
1924	4	568	1025	2477	3502
1925	4	509	1067	2600	3667
1926	4	519	1022	2485	3507
1927	4	538	918	2245	3163
1928	4	592	800	2114	2914
1929	4	584	773	2009	2782
1930	4	589	749	2199	2948
1931	4	595	768	2337	3105
1932	4	604	609	1605	2214
1933	4	581	637	1577	2214

direction either ran through or had through carriages to or from Ilfracombe. In the Down direction, there were also two excursion workings listed for Saturdays and one on Thursdays, the Thursday train and one of the Saturday excursions originating at Paddington. Excursion workings in the Up direction comprised one to London (Mondays and Fridays only), and two late on Friday evenings (one for London and 'the North via Midland Railway and Birmingham', the other 'for the North via Severn Tunnel, also G.C. Excursion Passengers via Banbury'). The same WTT also listed two freight workings in the Down direction (three on Mondays) and three in the Up direction, plus a number of goods workings traversing only part of the line (e.g.Taunton - South Molton). There were

no Sunday workings. The public timetables for July 1922 featured seven passenger trains each way on weekdays, five of which were 'all stations' services. The others stopped only at Wiveliscombe, Dulverton and South Molton, as did one additional Down train and three extra Up trains on Fridays only. (Fridays Only workings were marked as 'Third Class'). There was also a Saturdays only late-evening working from Taunton to Wiveliscombe, but no Sunday services were provided.

In those 1922 timetables, all but one train in each direction was effectively shown as working through to or from Ilfracombe, but the reality was a little different. Only three Down and two Up trains (four Down and five Up on Fridays) were actually through trains to or from Taunton, the others merely containing through carriages.

As for motive power, the usual GWR locomotives in early standard gauge days were 'Metro' 2-4-0Ts in conjunction with 2-4-0 and 0-6-0 tender engines. It is known that a steam railmotor was used between Taunton and Milverton from August 1908 to November 1928, Taunton shed having received railmotors Nos 26 and 71 in April and March 1908 respectively, initially for duties to and from Castle Cary.

The allocation lists reveal much about the motive power used on the Taunton - Barnstaple line, the 1909 register showing the following to be resident at Barnstaple shed:

'Metro' 2-4-0T: Nos 468 (from 11/9), 629 (all year), 630 (until 14/8), 632 (from 6/11), 1451 (only until 2/1) and 3590 (17/7 to 9/10).
'Standard Goods' 0-6-0: Nos 496 (until 4/12), 790 (11/9 to 9/10).
'Dean Goods' 0-6-0: Nos 2388 (17/7 to 14/8), 2466 (only until 2/1).
'1076' 0-6-0ST: Nos 1076 (30/1 to 27/2), 1587 (27/3 to 10/9 and from 6/11).
The official lists for 1920 showed the

Bishops Nympton & Molland, looking west towards Barnstaple, September 1964. All looks very neat, although the goods sidings (behind the Down platform on the right) had been lifted a few weeks before this picture was taken. PHOTO: ANDREW MUCKLEY

following to have been allocated to Barnstaple - once again, an average of three or four engines at any one time:
'Metro' 2-4-0T: Nos 456 (12/9 to end of year), 461 (until 28/3, and 15/8 to 10/10), 626 (1/2 to 29/3 and 23/5 to 20/6), 975 (until 1/2, also 29/2 to 23/5 and 20/6 to 7/11), 985 (23/5 to 20/6 and 18/7 to 7/11), 1456 (25/4 to 23/5), 1500 (25/4 to 23/5, 20/6 to 15/8, 7/11 to 5/12).
'Standard Goods' 0-6-0: Nos 504 (10/10 to 5/12), 704 (29/2 to 28/3), 1187 (25/4 to 23/5, 18/7 to 12/8).
'1076' 0-6-0ST/PT: Nos 959 (28/3 to 25/4), 1181 (until 1/2, and 14/6 to 10/10).
'1813' 0-6-0PT: Nos 1845 (25/4 to 20/6).
'Dean Goods' 0-6-0s: Nos 2381 (7/11 to 5/12), 2473 (29/2 to 28/3).
'3521' 4-4-0: Nos 3532 (10/7 to 7/11, 5/12 to end of year), 3548 (28/3 to 25/4), 3551 (23/5 to 18/7).

South Molton station, looking east towards Norton Fitzwarren, September 1964. This was the busiest intermediate station on the line. Its passing loop was extended in 1907 and lengthened in 1937, requiring the addition of timber-built extensions to the platforms (similar to some other stations on the line). In 1928 the Down line (on the right) was resignalled for working in both directions, partly to avoid the need for luggage and parcels from Up trains having to be carried across to the main platform. The goods yard is behind the Down platform, but although public goods facilities had been withdrawn a month before this picture was taken, the sidings were not taken out until 1965. PHOTO: ANDREW MUCKLEY

		SOUTH MOLTON			
	STAFF		RECEIPTS (£)		
Year	No.	Wages	Pass	Goods	Total
1903	12	492	4483	7412	11895
1913	9	545	4349	9331	14280
1923	9	1229	6867	15310	22177
1924	9	1234	6659	14353	21012
1925	9	1362	6370	15502	21872
1926	9	1320	6377	14029	20406
1927	9	1379	6477	14785	21262
1928	9	1384	6299	14331	20630
1929	10	2042	5984	15680	21664
1930	10	1553	5520	14623	20143
1931	10	1566	5024	14942	19966
1932	10	1395	4329	13576	17905
1933	9	1499	3686	12558	16244

South Molton station, looking east, 3 September 1960. Taunton Mogul No 6398 leaves with a mid-afternoon Barnstaple train.
PHOTO: E.T. GILL

Filleigh station, looking east towards Norton Fitzwarren, September 1964. The Down platform (on the right) and a new 42-lever signalbox (the second largest on the line) were added during the general improvements of 1937. The goods yard is behind the photographer and to the left - it once had a private siding and goods shed owned by the Fortescue Estate. PHOTO: ANDREW MUCKLEY

Filleigh station, looking west towards Barnstaple, 21 July 1964. The 10.40 Barnstaple Junction - Taunton train is hauled by Taunton 2-6-0 No 7337 which, at the time, had only two months left in service. PHOTO: ROGER PALMER

	FILLEIGH				
	STAFF		RECEIPTS (£)		
Year	No.	Wages	Pass	Goods	Total
1903	2	125	909	1200	2109
1913	2	131	1101	1356	2457
1923	3	472	2006	2304	4310
1924	3	452	1824	2222	4046
1925	3	439	1653	1888	3541
1926	3	426	1693	1786	3479
1927	3	413	1643	2196	3839
1928	4	442	1533	2283	3771
1929	3	440	1486	2259	3745
1930	3	491	1484	2659	4143
1931	3	454	1307	2391	3698
1932	3	419	1167	2719	3886
1933	3	415	1080	2958	4038

Swimbridge station, looking west towards Barnstaple, 1 August 1963. No 7304 waits with the 14.24 Barnstaple Junction - Taunton train. PHOTO: ROGER PALMER

Swimbridge station, looking east towards Norton Fitzwarren, September 1964. The Up loop and platform were added in 1904, although the goods shed was in situ before then. Note that the style of the station buildings differs to that of the other stations on the line - a smaller waiting room than usual on the main platform, but a brick-built shelter on the other platform. PHOTO: ANDREW MUCKLEY

At the start of 1921 (four-week period commencing 2 January), the shed's residents were 'Metro' Nos 461 and 985, 'Dean Goods' No 2570, and '3521' class 4-4-0 No 3547. The 4-4-0 was one of a class of forty which had started life in 1887/8 as 0-4-2Ts (twenty having been built as broad gauge convertibles), had been converted to 0-4-4Ts in the early 1890s, and had then been rebuilt as 4-4-0s in 1899-1902.

Moving ahead to 1 January 1934, Barnstaple shed had an allocation of three engines - 'Bulldog' 4-4-0s Nos 3416 JOHN W.WILSON and 3444 CORMORANT and '4300' class 2-6-0 No 4391 - while on 1 January 1948 '2251' class 0-6-0s Nos 2266 and 2275 were at Barnstaple. The depot was a sub-shed of Taunton (coded 'TN' in GWR days and 83B from 1950).

Of the engines shown on the 1934 allocation lists, No 3444 was one of at least three Taunton-based 4-4-0s which, in the late 1930s, had their tenders fitted with Whitaker Staff Apparatus to enable the train staff to be picked up more easily at speeds of up to 40mph. Other Taunton 4-4-0s known to have been simi-

larly fitted include No 3361 (formerly EDWARD VII) and No 3443 CHAFFINCH, which were nominally allocated to the parent depot of Taunton on 28 June 1937 and 11 February 1936 respectively, although No 3361 actually went to Barnstaple first. As a quick aside about 'Bulldogs' Nos 3443 CHAFFINCH and 3444 CORMORANT, the GWR hierarchy originally suggested to George Churchward that he name the two engines GIRAFFE and HAWK respectively, but Churchward over-ruled the suggestion.

The 2-6-0s, which became synonymous with the Taunton - Barnstaple line, were first used on the route in the mid-1920s. It was usual to find nine of the class allocated to Taunton for working, not only the Barnstaple line, but also to a lesser extent the Minehead branch, those more usually employed on the Barnstaple route having their steps reduced to an overall width of 8ft 4in to permit them to work through to Ilfracombe. At various times, Nos 4339, 4349, 4361, 6305, 6323, 6363, 6364, 6372 6383, 6398 and 7314 all ran with tenders fitted with Whitaker Staff Ap-

paratus. A total of fourteen '4500' and '5500' class 2-6-2Ts, six 'Dean Goods' and four '2251' class 0-6-0s were also equipped with the apparatus by 1937, the 0-6-0s being regularly used on the Barnstaple line.

The weakest sections of the Taunton - Barnstaple line were the two viaducts, and tests with a 'Hall' 4-6-θ in the late

	SWIMBRIDGE				
	STAFF		RECEIPTS (£)		
Year	No.	Wages	Pass	Goods	Total
1903	3	167	463	1096	1559
1913	3	195	630	1002	1632
1923	3	487	657	2244	2901
1924	3	428	607	2384	2991
1925	3	511	535	2244	2779
1926	3	469	502	1945	2447
1927	3	452	519	2564	3083
1928	3	429	557	2782	3339
1929	3	463	519	2912	3431
1930	3	513	467	3008	3475
1931	3	415	416	3036	3452
1932	3	424	427	2441	2868
1933	3	445	540	2552	3092

1940s proved that the class was rather too heavy to be passed for regular use over the structures. Nevertheless, different forms of motive power were sometimes seen on the line in the BR era, the most usual foreigners being the SR's 'N' ('Woolworth') Moguls or, occasionally, BR Standard 2-6-2Ts. In 1953 one regular duty was given to a former L&SWR 'T9' class 4-4-0.

Looking at the public timetables over the years, in March 1940 there were five services each way on weekdays (none on Sundays), three in each direction having through carriages to or from Ilfracombe; there was also an early morning return working between Taunton and Venn Cross. The average journey times were around 105 minutes. In May 1943 five weekday trains in each direction (plus the Venn Cross local) were shown once again, but the Ilfracombe carriages had been discontinued; apart from one Down train, all ran to or from Barnstaple Junction. There was an additional service each way on Saturdays. Moving on to November 1946, there were six trains advertised each way on weekdays, four of which in each direction had through carriages to or from Ilfracombe. The final GWR public timetable (6 October 1947 until further notice!) again showed six trains each way, four in each direction working through to or from Barnstaple Junction. The fastest journey time was 106 minutes.

Those timetables were, of course, not for the peak summer seasons and, furthermore, a couple were for the war period. However, a full-blooded summer season public timetable - the one for 13 June to 18 September 1955 - now springs readily to hand. It shows that on weekdays, there were seven Down and eight Up trains, and it apparently informed the public that all but one Down and three Up services worked through, to or from Ilfracombe. Once again, however, the facts were rather different. The origins of the six allegedly 'through' trains in the Down direction (i.e. the trains to which the through carriages were actually attached) on weekdays were:

Arrival Ilfracombe 10.52am; 6.25 ex-Yeovil Town.
Arrival Ilfracombe 1.48pm; 8.12 ex-Salisbury.
Arrival Ilfracombe 3.40pm; 9.00 ex-Waterloo.
Arrival Ilfracombe 5.56pm; 4.40 ex-Barnstaple Jct.
Arrival Ilfracombe 7.17pm; 1.00 ex-Waterloo.
Arrival Ilfracombe 9.04pm; 3.00 ex-Waterloo.

On weekdays, there was also an early morning service from Taunton to Dulverton and return. On Saturdays, there were twelve Down and thirteen Up

trains. Of the Down trains, five either worked through to Ilfracombe or had through carriages - one with through carriages from Paddington - while seven of the Up trains had originated at Ilfracombe with three others having through carriages from that resort. Of the Up trains, one was destined for Manchester (Exchange), another for Cardiff, and one for Wolverhampton. Journey times between Taunton and Barnstaple (Victoria Road) varied from around 90 to just under 120 minutes.

As has been pointed out to this humble scribe in no uncertain terms, much has

Swimbridge station, looking west, 21 July 1964. Taunton's No 7337 simmers while waiting to pull away with the 10.40 Barnstaple Junction to Taunton service. PHOTO: ROGER PALMER

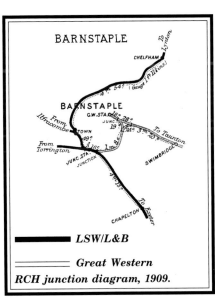

RCH junction diagram, 1909.

41

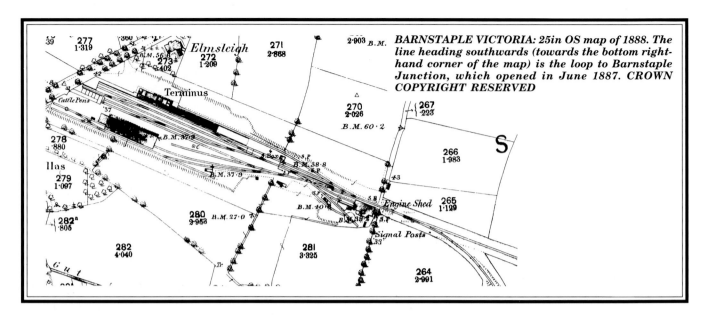

BARNSTAPLE VICTORIA: 25in OS map of 1888. The line heading southwards (towards the bottom right-hand corner of the map) is the loop to Barnstaple Junction, which opened in June 1887. CROWN COPYRIGHT RESERVED

been made elsewhere of GWR engines working to Ilfracombe with through trains off the Taunton - Barnstaple line. However, in the course of a whole year, they actually formed an almost insignificant proportion of the workings on the Barnstaple - Ilfracombe section.

The WTTs revealed a little more detail about the actual working of the line.

The WTT for winter 1947/48 stated that, on passenger duties, 2-6-0s were allowed 280 tons in either direction, although a footnote observed that the booked timings of passengers trains were based on a maximum of 230 tons. The loading restrictions stated that the 3306-3455 series of 4-4-0s, 44XX, 45XX and 55XX tanks, and most 0-6-0PTs

were permitted 220 tons, 3200 series 4-4-0s and '2251' 0-6-0s were allowed 190 tons, while 0-4-2Ts and the few remaining 'Metro' 2-4-0Ts had maximum loadings of only 120 tons.

Engine restrictions included the instructions that 'Blue' 2-6-2Ts were not permitted to work west of Wiveliscombe, and that engines fitted with ATC apparatus were not to work over the two wagon turntables at Barnstaple Junction yard unless their shoes were clipped up. The other restriction was the familiar requirement that engines working between Barnstaple and Ilfracombe had to have their steps cut back to a width of 8ft 4in.

The 'luxury' versions of the '4300' class 2-6-0s - the side-window cab '9300s' of 1932 - were heavier than their predecessors and, consequently, were classified as 'Red' engines. This effectively barred them from the Taunton - Barnstaple line. However, the modifying of the '9300s' in 1956-59 (to fill some of the gaps left by withdrawn '4300s') involved

GOODS TRAFFIC : BARNSTAPLE (GW)

Year	Forwarded			Received			Coal free	TOTALS	
	Coal	Mins	Goods	Coal	Mins	Goods		Tons	income
1903	12	120	6369	877	3113	11290	322	23103	14191
1913	3	1355	8176	185	1937	15312	867	27835	18822
1923	23	423	4019	199	2291	19419	5471	31845	35182
1924	-	556	3991	308	3952	20928	5394	35129	35682
1925	20	439	4184	123	4289	23373	3991	36428	35892
1926	20	535	3709	738	3454	22613	3436	34505	36372
1927	40	518	5813	249	3362	22704	4191	36877	41223
1928	58	701	6310	238	2513	24739	3401	37960	45634
1929	18	805	5774	247	3207	25849	4240	40140	46110
1930	25	1134	5247	245	3374	25488	4211	39724	43657
1931	-	539	4466	249	3857	25943	3856	38910	41603
1932	-	881	3397	281	3236	23695	3145	34635	36590
1933	11	825	3717	216	2848	23562	2306	33485	35980

PASSENGER TRAFFIC : BARNSTAPLE (GW)

Year	TICKETS		RECEIPTS (£)			
	Ord	Season	Pass	Pcls	Misc	Total
1903	32987	n/a	5579	1865	1584	9028
1913	26824	n/a	5265	2103	1359	8727
1923	28089	32	10819	1623	939	13381
1924	25427	21	10482	1481	840	12803
1925	26694	12	10768	1512	848	13128
1926	25494	41	11571	2335	666	14572
1927	23336	25	10628	2316	555	13499
1928	24211	37	10923	2325	612	13860
1929	22405	17	10662	2429	535	13586
1930	20388	35	9764	2435	873	13072
1931	17983	40	8897	2289	643	11829
1932	16536	31	7912	2247	441	10600
1933	15715	78	7820	2642	683	11145

BARNSTAPLE

Year	STAFF		RECEIPTS (£)		
	No.	Wages	Pass	Goods	Total
1903	35	2261	9028	14191	23219
1913	28	2195	8727	18822	27549
1923	33	5821	13381	35182	48563
1924	33	5171	12803	35682	48485
1925	33	5285	13128	38892	52020
1926	36	4814	14572	36372	50994
1927	36	5382	13499	41223	54722
1928	37	5429	13860	45634	59494
1929	38	5513	13586	46110	59696
1930	38	5531	13072	43657	56729
1931	38	5447	11829	41603	53432
1932	37	5274	10600	36590	47190
1933	37	5722	11145	35980	47125

Mogul No 6343 at Barnstaple shed - the building was originally broad gauge, hence its apparently generous dimensions. When it closed in 1951, locomotives and men were transferred to the SR premises at Barnstaple Junction. The '43XX' 2-6-0s were, for many years, synonymous with the Taunton - Barnstaple line.

a reduction in their weights, and after being reclassified 'Blue' engines they were permitted to work the Barnstaple line. In their rebuilt form, incidentally, they were renumbered 7322-7341.

Barnstaple (GWR) shed closed in January 1951, its locomotives and staff being transferred to the ex-SR depot at Barnstaple Junction. Otherwise, things remained little altered until the following decade. The former GWR station at Victoria Road in Barnstaple closed on 13 June 1960, and this necessitated the reopening of Barnstaple East Loop so that Taunton trains could work directly to and from Barnstaple Junction and Ilfracombe once again without having to reverse.

Prior to the changes of 1960, the usual practice had been for an engine arriving at Victoria Road station from Taunton to run round its train, then to haul the train tender-first to Barnstaple Junction, after which it went to the ex-SR shed for turning. On the return trip, the engine ran tender-first to Victoria Road, where it ran round the train and subsequently faced smokebox-first for the journey to Taunton. In the case of through trains from Taunton to Ilfracombe, the engine was uncoupled at Victoria Road and, after being replaced by a fresh engine, ran light to Barnstaple Junction to be turned. With the through trains from Ilfracombe to Taunton, the Ilfracombe engine hauled the train to Victoria Road, where it was replaced by a fresh steed.

On the Taunton - Barnstaple line, it was autumn 1964 before the inevitable diesel take-over, 2- or 3-car sets (or sometimes single cars) being most widely used on 'local' services with locomotive haulage on longer-distance through workings. Steam was, however, to have a final fling, the last known steam-hauled working on the line being a five-coach special on 27 March 1965, 0-6-0 No 3205 being in charge of proceedings. By then, goods traffic was a thing of the past, the stations along the line having been deprived of public goods facilities by mid-1964.

The Taunton - Barnstaple line was one of many which were earmarked for the Beeching axe, closure being proposed for August 1965, but the application of the Doctor's medicine had to wait as there were difficulties in organising the replacement bus services. The line officially succumbed on Monday 3 October 1966, the last trains having run on Saturday 1st. Nevertheless, the line between Barnstaple Junction and Victoria Road station (via the old South Loop) was retained so that the latter could still accommodate goods traffic, and this it did until 30 May 1970.

Barnstaple (GWR) station, undated. The track layout is slightly different to that shown on the OS map. The engine looks like a 'Dean Goods' fitted with a 'Standard Goods' outside-framed tender - it could be assumed that the train has recently arrived from Barnstaple Junction, as the engine has yet to run-round to face smokebox-first for the rest of its journey to Taunton. The wagon in the foreground is a Cordon - carrying gas for the replenishment of carriage lighting. PHOTO: JOHN SMITH

Barnstaple Junction shed, 24 May 1935. The 'E1Rs' were 0-6-2T rebuilds of LBSCR 0-6-0Ts. They were modified primarily for working on the Torrington - Halwill line, which opened in 1925, and it was usual to find six allocated to Barnstaple Junction at any one time. No 2610, which is shunting alongside the shed, was rebuilt in January 1929. Apart from a brief stay at Plymouth during the war, it remained at Barnstaple until its retirement (as BR No 32610) in March 1956. PHOTO: H.C. CASSERLEY

BARNSTAPLE to ILFRACOMBE

Ilfracombe is one of the less brash holiday resorts in the South West. It has been a popular resort since Victorian times, the June 1898 issue of *The Railway Magazine* offering this description of its attractions: '*A bold and broken shore of rocks has a back-ground of thickly-wooded glens, which in spring and summer are a paradise of flowers. In the town itself there is admirable accommodation for all classes of visitors, the hotels and boarding and lodging houses being as a rule alike commendable. Swimming may be enjoyed by ladies and gentlemen both from the rocks and in very commodious baths. The Capstone Hill, with its breezes, its winding walks, its music, its youth and beauty, is a never-failing source of recreation and pleasure*'.

The railway between Barnstaple and Ilfracombe was a little bit special. The route's appeal was, admittedly, partly due to its distinctive L&SWR/SR flavour, but it also had something else which is not easy to define. A description of a journey on the line is the ideal way of trying to recapture the essence of the route, but although this scribe travelled on the line several times in the 1950s and 1960s, there's little chance of him relying on his abysmal memory for specifics. Adopting the 'buck shifting' method instead, one of the more emotive accounts of a journey was featured in the *Railway Magazine* of July 1927 : '*Approaching Barnstaple Junction (from the direction of Exeter), the River Taw is crossed by a viaduct, and a good view is had of the bridge carrying the Great Western line from that company's station in Barnstaple, as it crosses the same river, which is here of fair width.*

'*Although somewhat on the outskirts of the town, Barnstaple Junction is the busiest station from the traffic point of view. On the down side there is an island platform, and, if there are local vehicles to go on with Torrington through coaches, it is usual for the latter to be taken from the rear of the Ilfracombe train on one platform line and transferred to the Torrington train on the other side of the island during the four or more minutes spent at the junction.*'

A later passage explained that: '*The method employed for attaching through coaches to a train of local stock at Barnstaple Junction is that the stock for Torrington - always at the rear of the trains from Exeter - is uncoupled, the Ilfracombe section sent away first, and the local stock (usually in charge of a 4-4-0 Adams locomotive) shunted on in front of the detached coaches, passengers and luggage being loaded up from the same platform. During the winter season the slip coach from the 'Cornish Riviera Ltd' is shunted on at Barnstaple Junction, in front of the 'Atlantic Coast' stock. This coach arrives some 30 minutes earlier than the 'Atlantic Coast' train at Barnstaple Junction.*

'*There is only one up platform, somewhat longer than the other, but, between, there is an up line, so that the Torrington train can be run through and placed in front*

The Taw Bridge, Barnstaple, 1 August 1952. 'West Country' Pacific No 34024 TAMAR VALLEY crosses the river at Barnstaple with the up ACE. PHOTO: R.E. TOOP

of an Ilfracombe portion occupying the platform.'

Post-war practice was for the Torrington train to arrive first, the engine to be uncoupled, and the station shunter to be attached to the rear of the carriages; they were then drawn back on to the Torrington line to permit the train from Ilfracombe to enter the station, the Torrington carriages then being attached to the rear of those from Ilfracombe.

'Adjacent to the station is the engine shed, goods yard, sidings etc. at the east end, and at the west end there is a sharp curve to the right round to Barnstaple Town station, while the Torrington line continues with a curve to the left as it follows the general course of the River Taw as far as Bideford. The Junction station, though somewhat old-fashioned, has refreshment room and other accommodation, and a good part of each platform is covered.

'Having detached the Torrington vehicles and added a Great Western through vehicle for Ilfracombe, another 2-6-0 had a load of 250 tons to take over the terrific gradients of the Ilfracombe branch, but not without assistance, as will be seen. Curving sharply round and passing several works and industrial premises, there is a short stretch of single line to cross the River Taw by a severely curved girder bridge carried on pillars sunk in the river bed. This bridge is close alongside the main road bridge, but curves round to

Barnstaple Town station. This has one main line platform only, with a terminal bay for Lynton and Barnstaple narrow gauge trains, all of which make connection with Ilfracombe line trains. As the station is alongside the river, a good view is had across its fairly wide stretches to the further bank, beyond which the Torrington trains can be seen if one is passing at the time.

'Leaving the station, Ilfracombe trains cross a swing bridge over the River Yeo as it runs into the Taw and the route then becomes double track, as it is all the way to Ilfracombe. For two or three miles the line follows the River Taw very closely, giving magnificent views of its sweeping stretches, right away, indeed, to Appledore and beyond to the open sea. Before reaching Wrafton, however, we turn inland. A short run then brings us to Braunton station. Here, a Drummond 0-4-4 tank, No.25, came behind to assist up the terrific bank, largely at 1 in 33 [sic], to Mortehoe, five and three quarter miles. On this stage, the line rises high among the hills, sometimes in cutting, sometimes overlooking wide stretches of hill country, with occasional glimpses of the distant sea. Inevitably, speed is slow, but the section is scenically attractive, and the fact that so steep a gradient is being mounted by adhesion adds special interest.

'The summit is just before Mortehoe station, where we leave No.25, also a fair

number of passengers for Woolacombe and Lee, both attractive resorts not far from Ilfracombe, but best reached by road from Mortehoe station. Then comes an equally fearsome descent, now with sections at 1 in 37 [sic], as the line continues its way down the valley, past a series of reservoirs in steps, until glimpses of the open sea and views overlooking the town of Ilfracombe, indicate the approach to the terminus which serves that attractive resort. The line is still high above the town, and the siding and other lines have their buffer stops apparently mounted on the edge of the seemingly precipitous mound upon which the well-built modern station is placed. Fortunately, however, there are abundant means of transport in the town, so that there is no imperative need for anyone to undertake the somewhat toilsome climb back to the station on foot'. Heady stuff indeed! The article from which that extract was taken actually referred to the River Taw as the River Torridge (oops!), but this assiduous scribe has put matters right. The locomotive at the head of the train in that account, incidentally, was 'Woolwich' 2-6-0 No 843 ('N' class, later BR No 31843).

Going back in time, Ilfracombe was featured in several early proposals (two in the 1840s and others in subsequent decades), but the town did not get its railway until 1874. The catalyst for the promotion of the Ilfracombe line was, to

Barnstaple Junction station, 21 July 1964. Mogul No 7306 - draws forward with empty stock from the 13.15 service from Taunton. The lines ahead of the engine lead to Bideford, Torrington and Halwill, those diverging behind leading to Barnstaple Town and Ilfracombe. PHOTO: ROGER PALMER

L&SWR Working Timetable, summer 1909.

72   1st JUNE to 30th SEPTEMBER, 1909, or until further notice.

ILFRACOMBE BRANCH.
FOR SPEED RESTRICTIONS SEE PAGES A, B, C & D.

This is a Single Line as between Barnstaple Junction and Pottington Signal Box, between which points it is worked under the Regulations for working Single Lines by the Electric Train Tablet Block system.

Self-acting Catch Points are situated on the Ilfracombe Line as follows:—
Between **Braunton and Headon Mill Crossing; Headon Mill Crossing and Mortehoe; Mortehoe and Ilfracombe.**

DOWN TRAINS—WEEK DAYS.

	STATIONS.	C 1 Mail and Goods.		2 Passengr A		3 Passenger A		4 Goods B		5 Pass. July, Aug & Sept. only		6 Condnl. Goods.		7 Passenger		8 Passenger		9 Passengr		10	
		arr.	dep.	arr.	dep.	arr.	dep.	arr.	dep.	arr.	dep.	arr.	dep.	arr.	dep.	arr.	dep.	arr.	dep.	arr.	dep.
M. C.	**Barnstaple Junction**	a.m	a.m. 5 10	a.m. ...	a.m. 8 23	a.m. ...	a.m. 1010	a.m. ...	a.m. 1016	a.m. ...	a.m. 11 8	p.m. ...	p.m. ...	p.m. ...	p.m. 1218	p.m. ...	p.m. 2 3	p.m. ...	p.m. 2 53	p.m. ...	p.m. ...
				After No.1 Up arr.		After No.3 Up arr.		After No.3 Up arr.		After Nos.4 or 5 Up arr.				after No.6 Up.		A fter No.8 10 or 11 Up.		After No. 13 or 15 Up.			
... 52	Barnstaple Town	5 13	5 14	8 26	8 28	10 15	10 19	10 24	11 11	11 12			12 21	12 23	2 6	2 7	2 56	2 58		
0 66	Pottington Signal Box		5 16		8 29		10 16	10 25	10 33	11 13				12 24		2 8		2 59			
4 79	Wrafton	5 23	5 24	8 35	8 36	10 22	10 23	10 42	10 47	11 19	11 20			12 30	12 31	2 14	2 15	3 5	3 6		
5 73	Braunton	5 27	5 29	8 38	8 40	10 25	10 27	10 49	11 0	11 22	11 24	12 10	12 10	12 33	12 35	2 17	2 19	3 8	3 10		
8 13	Headon Mill Crossing		5 35		8 46		10 33	B 11 6		11 30		12 16		12 41		2 25		3 16			
11 63	Mortehoe	5 44	5 45	8 55	8 57	10 42	10 44	11 16	11 22	11 39	11 41	12 26	12 31	12 50	12 52	2 34	2 36	3 25	3 27		
14 73	**Ilfracombe**	5 55	...	9 7	...	1054	...	1132	...	11 51	...	12 41	...	1 2	...	2 46	...	3 37	...	A.	

DOWN TRAINS—WEEK DAYS—Continued.

STATIONS.	11 Pass. July, Aug. and Sept. only		12 Passenger		13 Goods F	14 Pass. July, Aug. & Sept. only		15 Pass. July 10th to Sept. 25th inclusive.		16 Pass.		17 Pass. July, Aug. & Sept. only		18 Pass.		19 Passengr		20 Pass. Commencing July 10th.		21 Pass. July, Aug. and Sept. only		22 Passenger.	
	arr.	dep.	arr.	dep.	dep.	dep.	arr.	dep.	arr.	arr.	dep.	arr.	dep.	arr.	dep.	arr.	dep.	arr.	dep.	arr.	dep.	arr.	dep.
	p.m.	p.m.	p.m.	p.m.	p.m.	p.m.	p.m.	p.m.	p.m.	p.m	p.m	p.m.	p.m.	p.m.	p.m.	p.m.	p.m.	p.m.	p.m.	p.m.	p.m.	p.m.	p.m.
Barnstaple Jc.	...	3 23	...	3 40	4 0	...	4 22	...	4 48	...	5 20	...	6 3	...	6 41	7 11	...	7 49	...	8 6	...	8 40	
	After No. 16 Up arr.		After No. 14 Up arr.		After No. 17 Up.	After No. 17 Up arr.		After No. 18 Up arr.		After No. 18 Up.		After No. 19 Up.		After No. 19 Up.		After No. 20 Up arr.		After No. 20 Up.		After No. 20 Up.		After No. 21 Up.	
Barnstaple Town	3 26	3 28	3 43	3 45	4 4	4 25	4 27	4 51	4 53	5 23	5 25	6 6	6 8	6 44	6 46	7 14	7 15	7 52	7 53	9 8	9 10	8 43	8 44
Pottington S. Box	3 29			3 46	4 5		4 28		4 54		5 26		6 9		6 47		7 16		7 54		8 11		8 46
Wrafton	3 35	3 36		...	...	4 34	4 35		...	5 32	5 33	6 15	6 16		...	7 22	7 23	8 0		...		8 51	8 52
Braunton	3 38	3 40	3 53	3 55	...	4 37	4 39	5 1	5 3	5 35	5 37	6 18	6 20	6 54	6 56	7 25	7 27	8 1	8 3	9 18	9 20	8 54	8 56
Headon Mill Csg.	3 46		4 1		...		4 45		5 9		5 43		6 26		7 2		7 33		8 9		9 26		9 2
Mortehoe	3 55	3 57	4 10	4 13	...	4 54	4 57	5 18	5 20	5 52	5 54	6 35	6 37	7 11	7 13	7 42	7 44	8 18	8 20	9 35	9 37	9 11	9 13
Ilfracombe	4 7	...	4 23	...	...	5 7	...	5 30	...	6 4	...	6 47	...	7 23	...	7 54	...	8 30	...	9 47	...	9 23	...

UP TRAINS.—WEEK DAYS.

	STATIONS.	1 Passeng		2 Pass. July, Aug. & Sept. only		3 Passeng		4 Passenger		5 Passenger. July 12th to Sept. 27th inclusive		6 Passenger		7 Condnl. Goods.		8 Passenger.		9 Pass. July, Aug. & Sept. only		10 Pass. July, Aug. & Sept. only		11 Pass. Commencing July 10th.	
		arr.	dep.	arr.	dep.	arr.	dep.	arr.	dep.	arr.	dep.	arr.	dep.	arr.	dep.	arr.	dep.	arr.	dep.	arr.	dep.	arr.	dep.
M. C.		a.m	a.m	a.m.	a.m.	a.m.	a.m.	a.m.	a.m.	a.m.	a.m.	a.m.	a.m.	a.m.	a.m.	p.m.	a.m.	p.m.	p.m.	p.m.	p.m.	p.m.	p.m.
	Ilfracombe	7 30	...	8 0	...	9 15	...	9 52	...	G 10 15	...	G 11 0	...	11 30	...	11 55	...	G 12 17	...	1 0	...	1 20	
3 10	Mortehoe	7 40	7 41	8 10	8 12	9 25	9 26	10 2	10 4	10 25	10 28	11 10	11 11	11 40	11 47	...	11 55	12 27	12 30	1 10	1 11	1 30	1 31
6 60	Headon Mill Csg.	7 48		8 19		9 33		10 11		10 35		11 19		11 56		12 14		12 37		1 18		1 38	
9 00	Braunton	7 52	7 54	8 23	8 25	9 37	9 39	10 15	10 17	10 39	10 41	11 23	11 25	12 1	...	12 18	12 20	12 41	12 44	1 22	1 24	1 42	1 44
9 74	Wrafton	7 56	7 57	8 27	8 28	9 41	9 42	10 19	10 20	...	...	...	...	...		...	...	...	...	1 26	1 27	...	...
14 07	Pottington S. Box	8 3			8 34		9 48		10 26		10 48		11 32				12 27		12 51		1 33		1 51
		Aft. No. 1 Down.		After No. 2 Down.		After No. 2 Down.		After No. 4 Down.		After No. 4 Down.		After No. 4 or 5 Down.				After No. 7 Down.		After No. 7 Down.		After No. 7 Down.		After No. 7 Down.	
14 21	Barnstaple Twn	8 4	8 6	8 35	8 36	9 49	9 51	10 27	10 29	10 49	10 52	11 33	11 35			12 28	12 30	12 52	12 55	1 34	1 36	1 52	1 54
14 73	**Barnstaple Junction**	8 9	...	8 39	...	9 54	...	10 33	...	10 55	...	11 38	...	12 33	...	12 58	...	1 57	...	1 39	...	1 57	

UP TRAINS—WEEK DAYS.—Continued.

STATIONS.	12 Goods E July, Aug. & Sept. only.		13 Passenger June only.		14 Goods E June only.		15 Pass. July, Aug. & Sept. only.		16 Pass. July, Aug. & Sept. only.		17 Passngr.		18 Goods.		19 Passngr D		20 Pass.		21 Passngr. & Mails.		22 Pass.	
	arr.	dep.	arr.	dep.	arr.	dep.	arr.	dep.	arr.	dep.	arr.	dep.	arr.	dep.	arr.	dep.	arr.	dep.	arr.	dep.	arr.	dep.
	p.m.	p.m.	p.m.	p.m.	p.m.	p.m.	p.m.	p.m.	p.m.	p.m.	p.m	p.m	p.m.	p.m.	p.m	p.m	p.m	p.m	p.m	p.m	p.m	p.m
Ilfracombe	...	1 35	...	1 38	...	1 50	...	2 0	...	2 40	...	3 14			...	4 57	...	6 15	...	7 40	...	10 0
Mortehoe	1 45	2 22	1 48	1 49	2 0	2 15	2 10	2 12	2 50	2 52	3 24	3 25			5 7	5 8	6 25	6 26	7 50	7 52	10 10	10 11
	Shunt for No. 15 Up.				Pass. No. 12 Up.																	
Headon Mill Crossing	2 31		1 56		2 24		2 19		2 59		3 32				5 15		6 33		7 59		10 18	
Braunton	2 37	2 45	2 0	2 2	2 30	2 40	2 23	2 25	3 3	3 5	3 36	3 38			5 19	5 21	6 37	6 39	3 8	8 5	10 22	10 24
Wrafton	2 48	2 53	2 4	2 5	2 42	2 43	...	...	3 7	3 8	3 40	3 41			5 23	5 24	6 41	6 42	8 8	8 10	10 26	10 27
Pottington Signal Box	3 2		2 11		3 2		2 32		3 14		3 47		4 35		5 30		6 48		8 14		10 33	
	After No. 9 Down.		After No. 8 Down.		After No. 9 Down.		After No. 8 Down.		After No. 9 Down.		After No. 12 Down.		After No. 13 Down		Aft. No 16 Down.		After No. 18 Down.		After No. 19, 20 or 21 Down.		After No. 22 Down.	
Barnstaple Town	3 3	3 7	2 12	2 14	3 3	3 7	2 33	2 35	3 15	3 18	3 48	3 50	4 40	4 42	5 31	5 33	6 49	6 51	8 18	8 19	10 34	10 35
Barnstaple Junc.	3 10	...	2 17	...	3 10	...	2 38	...	3 21	...	3 53	...	4 43	...	5 36	...	6 54	...	8 21	...	10 38	...

Light Engines may be expected to run between Barnstaple and Ilfracombe at times uncertain and without previous notice.
A No. 2 Down will convey a L. and S.W. and No. 3 Down a G.W. Vacuum Goods Vehicle for Ilfracombe.   **B** Calls at Stoney Bridge Gates and Headon Mill Signal Box when required to put out stores.   **C** No 1. Down will convey Goods Wagons and Traffic to Ilfracombe, but only Road Box Traffic to other Stations. The Train must stop short of Shapland and Petters Crossing to enable the Porter, who will ride on the Engine from Barnstaple Junction, to alight and to take charge of the Gates while the Train passes.   **D** No. 19 Up will convey a L. and S.W. and a G.W. Vacuum Goods Vehicle from Ilfracombe for London.   **E** Calls at Duckpool Crossing when required to put out Stores.   **F** No. 13 Down to have two Vans, any Wagons for Rolles Quay to be placed between them.
G Stops at Mortehoe to take up Passengers only.

Barnstaple Junction station, 21 July 1964. Just a couple of months before its withdrawal, semi-anonymous 2-6-0 No 7306 marshals the empty stock from the afternoon train from Taunton. It is at the north end of the station, on the lines leading towards Bideford. PHOTO: ROGER PALMER

a great extent, the arrival at Barnstaple of the North Devon Railway, which opened its line throughout from Crediton to Fremington (just beyond Barnstaple) on 1 August 1854. By then, Ilfracombe had started to develop as a holiday resort, despite the

poor road communications over difficult terrain and the erratic scheduling of the seasonal steamer services.

The Barnstaple - Ilfracombe line was constructed by the logically named Barnstaple & Ilfracombe Railway, which had the support and the offer of a work-

ing agreement from the London & South Western Railway. Its Act of Parliament included the clause that: '....the Company shall not, without the consent in writing of Mr.William Westacott .... construct any portion thereof nearer to the north-eastern corner of the wall of the ship yard occupied by him than ten feet, nor nearer to the south-eastern corner of the same yard than forty-three feet'.

When the line was virtually completed, the obligatory Board of Trade inspection was made by Lieut-Col Hutchinson. It was dated 15 July 1874: The line.... 'was authorised to be constructed and worked as a light railway, and in consequence about five and three quarter miles have been laid with flat bottomed rails weighing 60lb per yard, and an iron swingbridge has been constructed with girders of sufficient theoretical strength to bear only the light class of engines which are intended to run on the line. In other respects the works are all of sufficient strength to remove it out of the category of "light railway".

The report continued for four pages, much of it appearing to have been written with a pen-nib made from an aggressive coil spring. Of the sections which are decipherable, it can be determined that apart from relatively minor requirements regarding certain

Barnstaple Junction station, 23 July 1962. '43XX' 2-6-0 No 6340 waits with the 14.24 to Taunton. The building on the right is the goods shed. PHOTO: ROGER PALMER

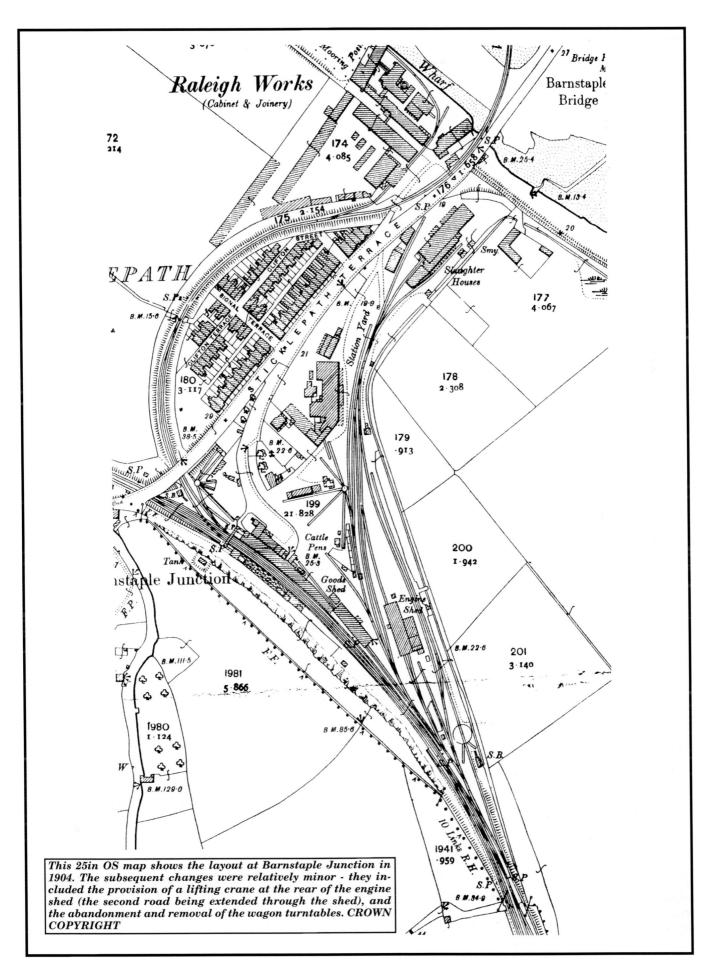

Raleigh Works
(Cabinet & Joinery)

This 25in OS map shows the layout at Barnstaple Junction in 1904. The subsequent changes were relatively minor - they included the provision of a lifting crane at the rear of the engine shed (the second road being extended through the shed), and the abandonment and removal of the wagon turntables. CROWN COPYRIGHT

Barnstaple Junction shed, 24 May 1935. 'E1R' 0-6-2T No 2135 and 'M7' 0-4-4T No 250. PHOTO: H.C. CASSERLEY

Barnstaple Junction shed, 21 July 1925. Adams 'Jubilee' 0-4-2 No 628 waits on the goods shed road (alongside platform 1 of the station), while Maunsell 'Woolworth' 2-6-0 No 860 stands adjacent to the coal stack. PHOTO: H.C. CASSERLEY

locks. At Barnstaple Town Station the iron hand-rail on the viaduct requires a little further extension. Owing to the subsidence of some of the embankments, the ballasting on them has become insufficient....'

A further observation was that: *'Judging from the amount of interchange traffic that takes place at Barnstaple (Old) Station [Barnstaple Junction] and from the fact that passengers arriving by down trains are allowed to cross the rails on their way to the town, it seems to me desirable that a footbridge or subway should be constructed at this station.'*

Before too long, the 'light railway' sections of the line were upgraded, Major-General Hutchinson (as he had, by then, become) inspecting the new works on 12 February 1887: *'The permanent way throughout the line has now been laid partly with steel rails and partly with iron double-headed rails, weighing 82lb and 75lb per yard respectively, secured to chairs weighing 40lb and 32lb each respectively, and it appears to be in good order.*

'The swing bridge has been strengthened and both theoretically and practically it is now strong enough to be crossed by heavy engines'.

Once again, the line was passed subject to certain alterations. This time, they included the resiting of the Up distant signal at Braunton station, the provision of check rails on some of the sharp curves, the electrical interlocking of the swing bridge over the Yeo at Barnstaple, and the reballasting of the line across five of the newly-strengthened over-bridges.

The route of the Barnstaple - Ilfracombe line was initially single, but doubling between Pottington Signal Box (just to the north of Barnstaple Town station) and Ilfracombe was completed by July 1891. Looking at the route in a little more detail, after leaving

improvements to signalling and interlocking, additional lineside fencing, and the provision of shelters at Braunton and Mortehoe stations, the Lieutenant-Colonel was generally satisfied. He recommended that, subject to the necessary improvements having been made, the line be sanctioned to open on 20 July. Public services indeed commenced on 20 July 1874, the railway company having decided against a special opening ceremony.

Nevertheless, it appears that the L&SWR didn't completely fulfil its part of the bargain. After a return visit to the line on 22 September, Lieut-Col Hutchinson reported that: *'At the swing bridge* (across the Yeo at Barnstaple) *the bolt, which gives the signalman at Barnstaple Town Station control of the bridge, does not sufficiently enter the bolt*

Barnstaple Junction shed, 21 July 1925. Duplicated Adams '460' 4-4-0 No 0475 reposes inside the newly-whitewashed shed. The engine was withdrawn the following year. PHOTO: H.C. CASSERLEY

Barnstaple Junction station, looking north, April 1960. The lines diverging to the left of West Signal Box head off towards Bideford, those to the right of the box leading to Ilfracombe. PHOTO: RAIL ARCHIVE STEPHENSON

Barnstaple Junction the first station was at Barnstaple Quay (renamed Barnstaple Town in 1886), just beyond the east end of the bridge over the River Taw. Quay station was more centrally situated than Barnstaple Junction, but was on a somewhat cramped site and was replaced on 16 May 1898 by a new station just to the north. The new station - also named Barnstaple Town (52ch from Barnstaple Junction) - was also used by the narrow gauge Lynton & Barnstaple Railway, of which, more later.

A short distance beyond Barnstaple Town the line crossed the River Yeo on the swing bridge which had regularly featured in the BoT reports, the 1887 one recording that the opening arrangements for the swing bridge were safe in character but 'rather slow in operation'. On the north-west bank of the Yeo, a siding branching off to Rolle's Quay was opened on 23 February 1881, the working instructions for the newly-unveiled siding stating that: *'There are two Annett's Locks fitted to the points leading into the siding, the key of one Lock is the Barnstaple and Braunton Train Staff, and the key of the other fits a Lock in the Barnstaple Quay Signal box, and cannot be withdrawn from there till all Signals (except the Up Starting signal) worked from that Box are locked at Danger.*

'An Engine or Train can only be sent to Rolle [sic] *Quay when the Train Staff for the Barnstaple and Braunton Section is at Barnstaple Station.*

'Whenever there are any Trucks at Barnstaple to be taken to Rolle Quay, or

Barnstaple Junction station, late 1940s. Bulleid 'West Country' Pacific No 21C105, not named BARNSTAPLE yet, arriving at Barnstaple Junction from Ilfracombe. The locomotive was transferred from Exmouth Junction to Barnstaple in 1947, and in May 1948 was renumbered 34005. PHOTO: R.S. CARPENTER

Below:- West Country Pacific 34003 PLY-MOUTH, heads south over the curves of the Taw River bridge. Photo:- Neville Stead.

Barnstaple Town station, looking towards Ilfracombe. The station was only a single-platform affair, the bank of the River Taw (immediately beyond the left of the frame) ruling out inexpensive expansion. There was, however, a bay at the rear of the platform, but that was used by narrow gauge Lynton & Barnstaple trains. PHOTO: JOHN L SMITH

at Rolle Quay to be brought away, *Mr Heather will send an Engine from Barnstaple for the purpose, accompanied by two men in charge, one to act as Guard, and the other as Shunter.'* The rates for haulage to or from Rolle's Quay (in addition to the ordinary rates to or from Barnstaple Station) were: bricks, tiles, lime, coal and coke - 4d per ton; grain, oil cake, artificial manures, timber, slates, etc - 6d per ton. General merchandise was priced at 1s per ton.

There was, incidentally, another rail-connected wharf on the River Yeo, on the south-east bank, a little above Braunton Bridge. It was served by a siding off the Lynton & Barnstaple line, and could accommodate vessels up to 200 tons, coal from South Wales being the main traffic. It fell into disuse in the 1920s.

On the Barnstaple - Ilfracombe line, the other intermediate stations were at Wrafton (5miles from Barnstaple Junction), Braunton (6miles) and Mortehoe (11¾m). Of those three stations, Wrafton was initially provided with a siding but no passing loop, and when the line was doubled it became a conventional twin-platform affair with two sidings at the south end of the Down platform. In later years (believed to be in the early 1950s) one of the sidings accommodated a pair of camping coaches. Braunton station was originally provided with a passing loop, but was remodelled with twin platforms when the line was doubled. It had a goods shed and sidings behind the Up platform, and sidings for banking engines alongside the Down line. The ascent from Braunton, which started at 1 in 74 and peaked at 1 in 40, commenced just to the north of the station. Mortehoe station was, until May 1902, spelt Morthoe and was suffixed 'for Lee and Woolacombe'; the more-familiar title of Mortehoe & Woolacombe was not applied until June 1950. The station was 600ft above sea level, and prior to the doubling of the line in 1891 was equipped with a passing loop.

From Mortehoe the line descended towards Ilfracombe, the gradient being a ferocious 1 in 36. The terminus at Ilfracombe (15 miles) comprised a single platform which was double-faced, a similar arrangement being retained after the station and yard were remodelled in the 1929. Alongside the station were several carriage sidings.

Ilfracombe's original timber-built engine shed was opposite the station platform. It was subjected to various

Braunton station, looking north towards Ilfracombe, late 1950s. Until the doubling of the Ilfracombe line in 1891, Braunton was merely a passing place. The banking engines for the climb to Mortehoe waited in sidings at the south end of the station. PHOTO: JOHN SMITH

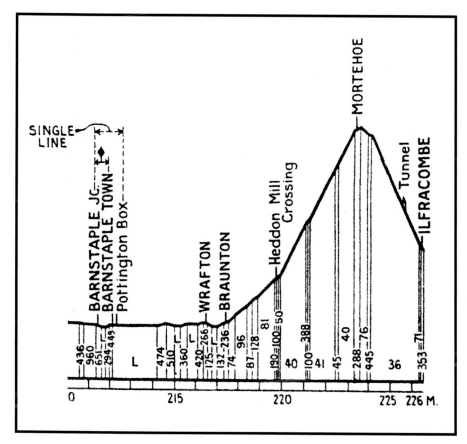

SINGLE
LINE

BARNSTAPLE JC.
BARNSTAPLE TOWN
Pottington Box

WRAFTON
BRAUNTON

Heddon Mill
Crossing

MORTEHOE

Tunnel
ILFRACOMBE

436
960
651
294 449

L

474
510
360

420 266
125
132 236
74
96
87-128
81
190 100 50
40
100 388
41
45
40
288-76
445-76
36
353 71

0   215   220   225 226 M.

modifications over the years, including the acquisition of Okehampton's old 42ft turntable in the late 1890s (the cost of a new one having been estimated at £1,100), a new rear wall in 1910 (a locomotive having demolished the original wall on 7 July), and a new siding and 120ft-long pit in 1911.

A completely new shed was erected in the late 1920s, a 65ft diameter turntable having been installed a few years earlier. This shed (built from the Southern's beloved 'Muribloc' concrete) and 'table were located just to the south of the station on a specially cleared site. The turntable was removed in 1964, by which time the introduction of diesel locomotives on the Ilfracombe line had rendered it superfluous. The shed was officially closed after steam workings ceased in 1964, but remained in use for some time as a diesel stabling point.

The parent depot of Ilfracombe shed was Barnstaple Junction. It is believed that the first engine shed at the site was owned by Thomas Brassey, the celebrated contractor who originally worked the Exeter - Crediton - Barnstaple line. The Bristol & Exeter Railway had anticipated securing a lease on the line, and the route had consequently been laid with broad gauge rails. However, the lease had been given, not to the B&ER, but to Brassey, and the latter therefore had

to provide broad gauge locomotives and rolling stock. The L&SWR obtained the lease on the line in 1863 (by which time it had been extended to Bideford), and standard gauge workings were introduced on 1 March of that year. Nevertheless, mixed gauge rails were retained until 1876 to give a daily B&ER coal train access to Bideford.

Little seems to be known about the fate of Brassey's engine shed and workshop at Barnstaple. In their extensively-researched tome *LSWR Engine Sheds*, (Irwell Press) Messrs. Hawkins and Reeve quote from an L&SWR minute of April 1863 which referred to: *'the present workshops at Barnstaple being no longer available for the purpose'.* However, a report which followed an inspection of locomotive facilities at Barnstaple in 1878 suggested: '.... *That the old engine shed at Barnstaple be examined and seen if worth repairs before any expense is incurred in removing it ...'* That remark almost certainly referred to the old Brassey shed, as the L&SWR's own shed was built by 1864. The conclusion is that although Brassey's buildings were not initially offered to the L&SWR, that company eventually took them over. A very sensible assumption.

The L&SWR shed was a barn-like structure built of timber, but with a slated roof. The roof was replaced in the inter-war years by one of corru-

gated iron and, apart from the provision of a small coal stage in 1874 - coaling having previously been undertaken from open trucks - and the installation of a larger turntable in the 1890s, minimal alterations were made to the shed and its facilities throughout the rest of its life.

Among the early occupants of Barnstaple Junction shed were William Beattie's 'Ilfracombe Goods' 0-6-0s, five of which were built by Beyer Peacock in 1873/74 and a further three by the L&SWR itself in 1875/80. These smart-looking locomotives had 4ft 6in diameter wheels and inside cylinders of 16in x 20in, and were intended primarily for freight duties on the new Barnstaple - Ilfracombe line, two of the class, Nos 282 and 283, actually hauling the first train on opening day. Two were scrapped in 1905, the other six being sold between 1910 and 1918 to Colonel Stephens' railways, the award for tenacity going to ex-L&SWR No 324 which, as Shropshire& Montgomeryshire Railway No 3 HESPERUS, was not formally condemned till 1941.

As a snippet of total irrelevance, HESPERUS had, in fact, been inactive at Kinnerley Junction (on the S&M) for some time prior to 1941, but when the War Department took possession of the S&M during the war, the Army's chief fitter (who had been trained by the LNER at Doncaster) proudly vowed that he would get the machine moving again. After a weekend's strenuous efforts the locomotive managed to raise steam, but none of the steam reached as far as the cylinders. Admitting defeat, the Army had HESPERUS towed away for scrap.

In the late 1890s Adams's 'T1' class 0-4-4Ts and 'Jubilee' class 0-4-2s started to appear at Barnstaple with increasing regularity, while Drummond's excellent 'M7' class 0-4-4Ts materialised in the 1900s. In true L&SWR/SR fashion, the 'M7s' enjoyed a lengthy association with Barnstaple. In January 1931 Nos 36, 242, 250 and 256 were allocated there, and by 1937 there were five of the class on the shed's books. The rosters of 1937 featured five 'M7' duties, including Barnstaple - Ilfracombe trips and Saturdays Only banking work at Mortehoe (two engines in summer). The allocation lists for mid-1951 show that eight 'M7s', Nos 30245, 30247, 30250, 30251, 30252, 30253, 30255 and 30256, were resident at Barnstaple while at the end of 1963 (a year after the Western Region had assumed control), Nos 30251, 30254 and 30670 were allocated there.

In 1925 a number of the versatile Woolwich-built 'N' class 2-6-0s were allocated to the Western Section of the SR, and by 1933 four were resident at

Ilfracombe shed, June 1935. An 'N' class Mogul simmers outside the 'new' engine shed of 1929. Photo:- W.A.Camwell.

Barnstaple Junction. Although they established a long residency in North Devon, by the summer of 1950 only one, No 31842, was shown on Barnstaple's complement. Nevertheless, sundry 'N' allocations continued until the end of 1956.

For the newly-opened line between Torrington and Halwill, seven Adams-designed '460' class 4-4-0s were transferred to Barnstaple Junction shed in July 1925, albeit with three of them usually outstationed at Torrington. During the summer season, they were also used on the Barnstaple - Ilfracombe line. On their intended stamping ground of the Halwill line, the 4-4-0s performed reasonably well, but when Halwill station was busy, access to the turntable was difficult. Replacements were therefore required, and in a bout of lateral thinking the Southern's CME, Richard Maunsell, decided to rebuild ten of the ex-LB&SCR 'E' class 0-6-0Ts as 0-6-2Ts.

The rebuilds were designated 'E1R', and underwent the necessary surgery in 1927-29. Subsequently, six were usually allocated to Barnstaple Junction at any one time, and remained there until being gradually displaced by LMR 2-6-2Ts as from 1953. Barnstaple shed's first Ivatt 2-6-2T was No 41298, which arrived in North Devon for work on the Halwill line in the summer of 1953. As for the displaced 'E1Rs', three went to Plymouth Friary (although not simultaneously), but one of the rebuilds, BR No 32696 clung on at Barnstaple where it was used mainly on local goods and carriage shunting duties.

Returning again to the pre-Nationalisation period, the November/December 1945 issue of *The Railway Magazine* included a report by two correspondents concerning the arrival of Bulleid's lightweight 'West Country' Pacifics on the Ilfracombe line: '.... *one of the new series signalised its arrival at Ilfracombe by blowing off with vigour, and with the help of 280lb pressure, lifted some of the glass from the station roof .... the new Pacifics are permitted to take a maximum of 8 bogies (about 260 tons tare) up the 1 in 36 from Ilfracombe to Mortehoe, as compared with the maximum of 180 tons allowed with the Moguls'.* Frequently, though, the Bulleid Pacifics were used to haul trains of just two or three coaches on the Ilfracombe line.

During the early days of the Pacifics, a 'West Country' proved unable to re-start a trial train of ten empty coaches on Mortehoe Bank, but succeeded with eight. In later years the official maximum loadings for the class were eight coaches from Braunton to Ilfracombe and seven in the reverse direction, but local crews were adamant that those loadings were manageable only when the rails were perfectly dry. The speed limits imposed on the Pacifics were: Barnstaple Junction - Braunton 55mph, Braunton - Mortehoe 40mph, and Mortehoe - Ilfracombe 30mph.

The Bulleid Pacifics remained a common sight in North Devon until late 1964, although the rebuilt versions were prohibited from the North Devon and Cornwall lines. In their rebuilt form they were devoid of the air-smoothed casing (Oliver Bulleid positively

loathed the word 'streamlining'), but their axle weights had been increased from 18tons 15cwt to 20tons 18cwt - hence the prohibition. An interesting little snippet in the February 1959 issue of *Trains Illustrated* observed that, during the previous Christmas period, several Nine Elms Pacifics had been noted working west of Exeter. Among them were Nos 34006, 34093, 34094, and 34095, while No 34098 TEMPLECOMBE, of Bournemouth (71B) had been seen leaving Exeter on 27 December with the Ilfracombe portion of the 1.0pm ex-Waterloo.

Under BR auspices Barnstaple Junction shed was coded 72F, and when the ex-GWR engine shed at Victoria Road in Barnstaple closed in January 1951, the latter's locomotives and staff were transferred to Barnstaple Junction. The shed became WR property at the beginning of 1963, and was recoded 83F from the end of that summer, by which time the WR was busy acting on its policy to eliminate steam traction west of Exeter.

The railway served Ilfracombe well. In its early days it did much to regenerate an ailing holiday trade, and by 1909 the summer schedules included seventeen trains each way on weekdays and three on Sundays. By the summer of 1922 there were fourteen passenger trains advertised on the Barnstaple - Ilfracombe line each way on weekdays (but no Sunday service), the timetables including a through carriage between Brighton and Ilfracombe on one train each day. Freight workings were sporadic, the WTTs usually including only

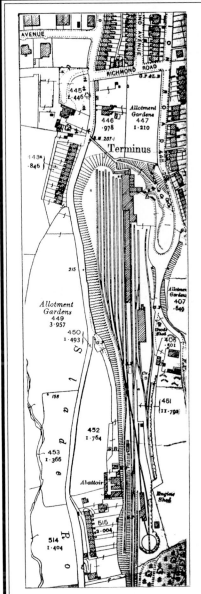

The 'new' post - 1929 layout at Ilfracombe is seen in this 25in OS map. CROWN COPYRIGHT

one or, at most, two trains in each direction on weekdays, although annotations sometimes referred to one or two passenger trains from Exeter operated as mixed trains between Barnstaple Junction and Ilfracombe.

Although the Barnstaple - Ilfracombe line was one of the more extreme outposts of the SR empire, it nevertheless hosted two named trains. The first was the 'Atlantic Coast Express', inaugurated on 19 July 1926. An in-house competition had been held to find a name for the long-standing 11am Waterloo - West of England service, and 'Atlantic Coast Express' had been the winning entry. For the record, that entry had been submitted by a guard at Waterloo who had won three guineas

for his creative thinking, the two runners-up each receiving a paperweight in the form of a 'King Arthur' 4-6-0. It's a fair bet that, in terms of monetary value, the paperweights are now worth a smidgin more than three guineas.

The 'ACE' was a multi-portioned working, with carriages appended for various destinations. The formation and scheduling of the train was far too involved to cover in this modest tome, and so it is perhaps appropriate to raise a cheer for D.W. Winkworth's excellent book *Southern Titled Trains* which goes into the subject in detail. In a nutshell, though, the through 'ACE' coaches for Ilfracombe and Torrington (usually a pair of brake composites) were taken from the front of the train at Exeter Central where a third coach was added. On reaching Barnstaple the Torrington coach was taken off, leaving the other two to continue their journey to Ilfracombe. The 'ACE' ceased operating as from 6 September 1964.

A contemporary account of the working of the 'ACE' (entitled 'To Ilfracombe by Atlantic Coast Express') appeared in the *Railway Magazine* of July 1927:*'In the summer there are normally two trains on ordinary weekdays and four or five on Saturdays. The 11am proper makes its first stop at Salisbury in 90 minutes and the next at Exeter (Queen Street). It is there divided, the first portion leaving at 2.21pm and runs to Barnstaple Junction. A further division then takes place, the main train, with through restaurant car, serving all stations onwards to Ilfracombe.*

'In the opposite direction the standard "Atlantic Coast Express" leaves Ilfracombe at 10.22am .... Mention may also be made of the through train from Brighton at 11.30am with through carriages to Ilfracombe (due 7.5pm), and the return train from Ilfracombe at 11.15am, which reaches Brighton at 6.31pm. Our return journey between London and Ilfracombe was made by "Atlantic Coast Express" near the end of the season, so that the number of passengers from London was not very great....'

The other named train to serve Ilfracombe was the 'Devon Belle', an all-Pullman affair inaugurated on 20 June 1947. The train initially ran only on Fridays, Saturdays, Sundays and Mondays, but between 1948 and 1951 a Down working on Thursdays and an Up service on Tuesdays were added; for 1952-54, there were services in both directions on Saturdays and Sundays, plus a Down train on Fridays and an Up working on Mondays.

The 'Devon Belle' had portions for Plymouth (usually only four carriages) and Ilfracombe and carried, at its rear, a 27-seat observation saloon. At Ilfracombe,

the saloon was turned on the locomotive turntable. The Ilfracombe portion of the 'Belle' comprised up to ten carriages but, as already mentioned, even a Bulleid Pacific couldn't haul that little lot up Mortehoe Bank on its own. Consequently, banking assistance was provided by 'N' class 2-6-0s or 'M7' 0-4-4Ts (sometimes in multiple) or even another Pacific. The 'Devon Belle' had only a brief life, the Plymouth portion being discontinued in 1949 and the Ilfracombe portion making its last journey on Sunday 19 September 1954.

The public timetables for the summer of 1952 advertised the following 43 comings and goings at Ilfracombe on Saturdays:

6.43am ex-Waterloo (through carriages)
7.40am to Taunton (via WR route)
7.42am ex-Waterloo (through carriages)
8.10am to Waterloo
8.25am ex-Taunton (via WR route)
8.46am ex-Barnstaple Junction
9.00am to Waterloo
9.25am to Cardiff (via WR route through Taunton)
10.12am to Taunton (via WR route)
10.14am ex-Taunton (via WR route)
10.30am to Waterloo ('Atlantic Coast Express')
10.55am to Birmingham (via WR route through Taunton)
10.57am ex-Yeovil Town
11.18am ex-Taunton (via WR route)
11.30am to Waterloo
12.00 to Waterloo ('Devon Belle')
12.09pm ex-Yeovil Town
12.35pm to Waterloo
1.27pm ex-Waterloo (through carriages)
1.45pm to Waterloo
2.05pm ex-Exmouth
2.10pm to Waterloo
2.21pm ex-Salisbury (until 30 August only)
2.41pm ex-Waterloo (through carriages)
2.55pm to Exeter (through carriages to Waterloo)
3.22pm ex-Waterloo (through carriages)
3.40pm ex-Waterloo (through carriages)
3.56pm ex-Taunton (via WR route)
4.36pm ex-Waterloo ('Atlantic Coast Express')
4.48pm to Exmouth
5.10pm ex-Paddington (via Taunton and WR; until 6 September only)
5.15pm to Taunton (via WR route)
5.27pm ex-Waterloo ('Devon Belle')
5.45pm to Barnstaple Junction
5.56pm ex-Portsmouth
6.16pm ex-Wolverhampton (via Taunton and WR route)

Ilfracombe station circa 1912. The original engine shed, replaced in 1929, can be seen to the right of the station. The 'M7' (L&SWR No.22, ultimately BR No. 30022) mysteriously displays the headcode for a Torrington working, the code for an Ilfracombe working being the diamond on the right and the disc on the left. PHOTO: LENS OF SUTTON

Ilfracombe station, early 1960s. 'N' class 2-6-0 No.31832, complete with Exmouth Junction shedplate, waits on what appears to be a wet day. Rain in North Devon - 'fraid so! PHOTO: JIM DAVENPORT

Ilfracombe, looking towards the dead-end, circa 1922. 'M7' No 251 (later BR No 30251) pulls away from the station with an Ilfracombe working, displaying the correct headcodes. The goods shed (on the right) survived the rebuilding of 1929, but the signalbox did not. PHOTO: R.S. CARPENTER

6.42pm ex-Exmouth
6.50pm to Taunton (via WR route; until 6 September only)
7.17pm ex-Waterloo (through carriages)
7.45pm to Exmouth
8.10pm to Taunton (via WR route)
8.30pm to Barnstaple Junction
9.08pm ex-Waterloo

At Ilfracombe, the usual practice was for arrivals to use No 1 platform (the longer face of the island platform) as it was equipped with run-round facilities, departures usually leaving from No 2 - the shorter platform face. There was another interesting working on the line - a 10am departure from Mortehoe for Waterloo, the starting point possibly chosen to provide returning holiday-makers with a nice empty train. With only very few exceptions, the workings listed above were 'all stations' services between Barnstaple and Ilfracombe, the small number of non-conformists omitting the Wrafton stop. Furthermore, it is worth pointing out that the Up 'ACE' ran non-stop through Barnstaple Junction.

As a final word on the above list of 1952 services, the trains to and from Taunton via the WR route had been a feature of the timetables since the earliest days, and since at least 1917 had sometimes been worked through to and from Ilfracombe by GWR engines and guards. In later years, the locomotives were usually '4300' and '6300' class 2-6-0s which, of necessity, had had their steps cut back to a maximum width of 8ft 4in.

The last day of regular steam working on the Barnstaple - Ilfracombe line was 5 September 1964, which was also the date for the last ever trip of the 'Atlantic Coast Express'. The diesel replacements were WR 'Warships' (which had been displaced from express duties by 'Westerns') and occasionally 'Hymeks' or North British 'Type 2s', with a fair smattering of multiple units.

During the 1960s the traffic figures on the Ilfracombe line declined, goods traffic ceasing with the conversion to DMU working on 7 September 1964. As an economy measure the line was singled in December 1967, but many of the overheads incurred by maintenance simply could not be reduced. The Exeter - Barnstaple line was treated to a government grant in 1969 but, ominously, the Ilfracombe section was denied financial assistance, and it came as little surprise when closure was announced. The date of execution was Monday 5 October 1970, the last trains having run the previous Saturday. The rails were lifted in 1975.

Below:- Ilfracombe station, August 1953. A Taunton train, with 2-6-0 No 6372 in charge, waits in the bay at Ilfracombe. The goods shed is on the right. PHOTO: R.S. CARPENTER

Classic L&B Manning Wardle 2-6-2T No. E760 EXE waits at Woody Bay station with a Barnstaple-bound train in the early 1930s. The oval SR numberplate on the rear of the cab had previously been worn on the cab side.

Barnstaple Town station, early 1930s. No E760 EXE prepares to take on water before coupling up to the front of its train.
PHOTO: E.R. MORTEN

58

LYNTON and BARNSTAPLE RAILWAY

Despite having closed almost 60 years ago, the Lynton & Barnstaple Railway is still remembered as one of the West Country's most charismatic little lines. Much has been written about it - not all of it totally accurate - and a wealth of preserved L&BR documentation is still waiting to be studied. Unfortunately, the publishers of this book have declined to make 500 pages available for a 'new and complete' history of the L&BR, and so the following is only a very brief account of selected aspects of the little railway's existence.

The L&BR's entry in 'Bradshaw's Shareholders' Guide' gave the basic facts: 'Incorporated by Act of 27th June 1895, for making a railway from Barnstaple to Lynton. Length, 19 miles 1 furlong 5 chains. Gauge, 1 foot 11½ inches'. The railway was primarily intended to tap tourist traffic to and from the twin beauty spots of Lynton and Lynmouth, the gauge of 1ft 11½in dictated mainly by the difficult nature of the terrain which the line was to cross although, of course, the reduced expense of narrow gauge construction was not ignored.

In May 1898 - shortly before the opening of the line - the L&BR's Chairman, Sir George Newnes, was the subject of an interview in *The Railway Magazine.* Sir George opined that, until then, Lynton and Lynmouth had been the only major tourist spots in England which were all of twenty miles from any railway station. He explained that: '....*it has been a regular thing in July and August to see twenty or thirty coaches and chars-a-banc from Ilfracombe crowd into Lynton between 11 and 12 o'clock in the morning, and the Directors naturally regard this traffic as likely to be a considerable source of revenue to the new Company. Almost by the time these words are in print the iron horse - or perhaps I ought to say the iron pony - will be journeying every day to the Switzerland of England, so that tourists from Ilfracombe will only have to ride by coach to Blackmoor, fully half the distance* (the Blackmoor - Lynton section) *being accomplished by rail...*

'....*At Blackmoor commodious stables are being built, as it is hoped the coaches will not run on to Lynton after the railway is opened. The horses will thus be saved the heaviest portion of the road. Through fares from Ilfracombe to Lynton are under consideration'.*

Apart from the Ilfracombe - Lynton horse buses, there were also buses to Lynton and Lynmouth from Barnstaple (a three hour trip in a twenty-seat vehicle), Minehead and Dulverton. In the mid-1890s, those three services had carried almost 30,000 passengers annually. During the interview with *The Railway Magazine,* incidentally, Sir George did not waste the opportunity of sounding off about one of his hobby-horses - the 'extortionate' prices which had sometimes been asked for land.

It seems that North Devon was a popular subject for *The Railway Magazine* in 1898. The June issue featured a report on the attractions of nearby Ilfracombe, the article including a comment or two about the L&BR which had, by then, opened: '*Among the numerous places around Ilfracombe to which visitors go in considerable numbers during the summer season, Lynton and Lynmouth hold the premier position. Hitherto these sylvan little retreats have been approached chiefly by coach, but quite recently a narrow gauge line like the*

Barnstaple Town station, 11 May 1931. L&B trains used the rear of the platform at Barnstaple Town, the SR line being hidden by the platform itself. The legend on the other side (i.e. the SR side) of the station nameboard proclaimed 'Change here for Lynton & Lynmouth'.

Barnstaple Town station, looking towards Lynton, pre-1922. The narrow gauge siding diverging to the left beyond the end of the platform led to a transfer bay, where goods were exchanged with the L&SWR. The latter's lines can be seen curving away to the left, in the mid-distance.

Festiniog in North Wales has been successfully launched. It runs from Barnstaple, and, though it is primarily intended for passengers, it will afford valuable facilities for the carriage of manure....'

Returning to the L&BR's gestation, the construction of the line was a traumatic affair. The contractor, James Nuttall of Manchester, eventually realised that the railway company's estimates (which he had accepted) had been somewhat optimistic, and he took the L&BR to court to try to recoup his additional expenditure. The judgement went for Nuttall, but the L&BR successfully appealed for a reversal of the verdict. Nuttall's response was to hand over the business to his son, and that left the company with no contractor, an unfinished line and, partly because of the court costs, more or less bare coffers. The L&BR subsequently completed the line itself.

The timing of James Nuttall's departure from the scene was agonisingly close to the projected completion date, a minute from the L&BR's half-yearly meeting of 24 February 1897 not-

ing that: *'The Chairman (Sir George Newnes).... stated that the construction of the line was being proceeded with. He was sorry to say the Contractor had applied for an extension of time to 1st July,*

and had asked the Directors to waive the penalty clause, but the Directors had written refusing to accede .... The Contractor has now put on extra men and promised to get the line completed at the

Pilton Yard, Barnstaple, pre-1923. The Baldwin 2-4-2T LYN nestles inside the shed, while one of the 2-6-2Ts is being prepared outside. The buildings on the right of the engine shed are the L&B's carriage sheds.

Above:- Pilton Yard, Barnstaple, mid-1920s. The L&B's Baldwin 2-4-2T LYN - clearly not of British origin - displays the first post-grouping arrangement of SR number-plates on the cab sides and name-plates on the tanks.

Middle:- Pilton Yard, Barnstaple, 16 May 1898. On the first day of public services on the L&B, well-polished 2-6-2Ts YEO and EXE, plus assorted staff, pose for the official snap.

Below:- Chelfham viaduct, August 1933. The elegant viaduct, some of its arches 70ft above the Stoke Rivers Valley, still stands today. It now has the status of a listed structure, but it has been suggested that, had it not been for the buildings underneath, it would have been demolished long before the days of 'listing'.

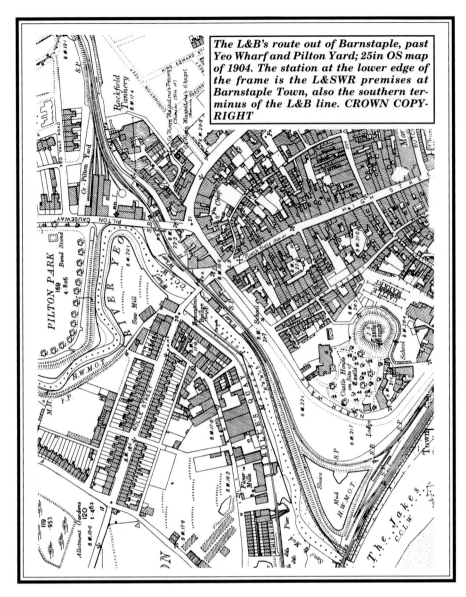

The L&B's route out of Barnstaple, past Yeo Wharf and Pilton Yard; 25in OS map of 1904. The station at the lower edge of the frame is the L&SWR premises at Barnstaple Town, also the southern terminus of the L&B line. CROWN COPYRIGHT

earliest possible moment. 'Contracts for the Locomotives, Rolling Stock and Signalling and Telegraph Apparatus have been entered into, and the Chairman was glad to say that in every case the amounts of the Contracts were rather under than over the Estimates. With regard to Land Purchases, however, the Directors had had to pay about three times as much as was originally estimated owing to the extravagant prices asked by the Land Owners. The Chairman also pointed out that the Directors, in view of possible increase of traffic in the future, had deemed it prudent to purchase sufficient land to make a double line of Railway throughout.

'Mr Jeune .... stated that he had yesterday gone over the Viaduct at Chelfham by train with 110 men and 28 trucks of earth, and he was glad to say there was not the slightest sign of deflection. The line from Barnstaple to Chelfham was now actually made, and trains could shortly be run to Bratton, a distance of about 12 1/2 miles. In about five weeks the

line to Parracombe was to be absolutely ready, and all the big works by the middle of April. The Contractor now promised to have men working night and day and that everything should be ready for the Board of Trade Inspection by about the 12th June'.

The intention was for the Lynton and Barnstaple to be provided with facilities at the L&SWR station at Barnstaple but, for a while, things did not go to plan. L&BR Directors' meeting, 9 July 1896: 'Resolved that, having regard to the difficulty in the negotiation with the LSWR Co as to the building of the Barnstaple Railway Station, arrangements be made for the station accommodation necessary for the Lynton Company being built and provided on their own land and that the Chairman be requested to write to Sir Charles Scotter (the L&SWR's Chairman) expressing the views of the Board'.

The L&BR's threat of building its own station worked, the outcome being that the L&SWR built a new station,

Barnstaple Town, for joint use. It cost around £6,000.

For those unfamiliar with the area, it should be explained that the 'twin' communities of Lynton and Lynmouth are separated by daunting cliffs, the former being on top of the cliffs and the latter nestling in the valley below. There was - and still is - a direct means of transport between the two in the form of a cliff railway, but that's another story. The possibility of the L&BR entering Lynmouth was totally out of the question, but a terminus at Lynton was a perfectly adequate alternative. That said, the siting of the station at Lynton was far from ideal. Although the railway company wanted to build in the middle of the town the owner of the necessary land refused to sell, and the station was therefore built to the south of the town, and some 250ft above it.

Apart from the inconvenience to passengers, the siting sometimes proved troublesome for the L&BR in another way. There existed what can be described as over-efficient drainage and, consequently, a reliable water supply was not one of its features. The town's reservoir was at a lower level, and the local water company required a hefty sum for connection and pumping. The alternative was for the L&BR to tap a spring on Dean Steep, some 1 1/2 miles away, but that spring frequently dried up in hot weather. Consequently, it became common practice for additional water tanks to be brought up from Barnstaple by rail during prolonged dry periods.

Over the years, the subject of Lynton station's water supply and drainage came under regular discussion, among the minutes being: Board meeting, 16 April 1912: 'Considered and Approved .... Revised scheme for dealing with Lynton station drainage by filtering tanks to be constructed on L&B Co's property adjoining signal cabin at estimated cost of £17'. A Board meeting of 19 December 1919 resolved that: 'the company purchase for the sum of Ten Pounds plus legal costs the existing water supply for Lynton Station, originating on Ribsworthy Farm'.

Returning once again to the formative years of the L&BR, the question of an access road to the station was discussed at length. The company's Engineer, Frank Chanter, compiled his report on the proposed road on 11 April 1896:

'(1) Several routes have been proposed for this road and no settlement has yet been made as so many points have to be considered for and against each scheme.

'(2) As requested by the Board I have enquired into the matter and also examined the surveys made of the various routes and the localities of each.

Southern Railway WTT for July 1932.

LYNTON AND BARNSTAPLE BRANCH.

Distances M.	C.	DOWN TRAINS. WEEK-DAYS ONLY.	Pass. and Mail. C arr.	dep.	Pass. arr.	dep.	Pass. arr.	dep.	NFSQ Pass. (18th JULY to 8th SEPTEMBER only.) arr.	dep.	Pass. A arr.	dep.	Pass. B arr.	dep.	Pass. arr.	dep.	Pass. B arr.	dep.
			a.m.	a.m.	a.m.	a.m.	a.m.	a.m.	a.m.	a.m.	p.m.	p.m.	p.m.	p.m.	p.m.	p.m.	p.m.	p.m.
...	...	Barnstaple (Pilton Yd.)	...	5†20	...	6†45	...	9†55	...	...	...	1† 5	..	2†55	...	4 † 5	...	
...	...	Barnstaple Town	5†22	5 33	6†47	7 0	9†57	10 15	...	11 3	1† 7	1 33	2†57	3 15	4 † 7	4 30	...	7 50
...	30	Barnstaple (Pilton Yard)	5	35	7	2	10	17	11	5	1	35	3	17	4	32	7	52
2	55	Snapper Halt	5 44	5 44½	7	11	10 26	10 27	11 14	11·14½	1 44	1 45	3 26	3 27	4 41	4 42	8 1	8 1½
4	55	Chelfham	5 52½	5 53	7	19	10X35	10 37	11 22½	11 23	1X53	1 55	3 35	3 36	4X50	4 51	8 9½	8 10
7	54	Bratton Fleming..........	6 6	6 6½	7 31	7 32	10 50	10 51	11 36	11 36½	2 8	2 9	3 49	3 51	5 4	5 5	8 23	8 24
11	62	Blackmoor	6 23½	6 24	7X49	7 50	11 8	11 9	11 53½	11 55	2 26	2 28	4X 8	4 11	5 22	5 24	8X41	8 43
14	34	Parracombe Halt	6 36	6 36½	8	1	11 21	11 22	12 7	12 8	2 40	2 42	4 23	4 24	5 36	5 37	8 55	8 55½
15	78	Woody Bay	6 44½	6 45	8	8	11 30	11 32	12 16	12 17	2 50	2 52	4 32	4 34	5 45	5 46	9 3½	9 4½
17	36	Caffyns Halt................	6 52	6 52	8	14	11 39	11 40	12 24	12 25	2 59	3 0	4 41	4 42	5 53	5 54	9 11½	9 12
19	23	Lynton	7 0	...	8 21	...	11 48	...	12 33	...	3 8	...	4 50	...	6 2		9 20	

Distances M.	C.	UP TRAINS. WEEK DAYS ONLY.	Pass. arr.	dep.	Pass. arr.	dep.	Pass. E arr.	dep.	Pass. B arr.	dep.	Pass. D arr.	dep.	Pass. arr.	dep.	Pass. B arr.	dep.	Pass. B arr.	dep.
			a.m.	a.m.	a.m	a.m.	p.m.	p.m.	p.m.	p.m.	p.m.	p.m.	p.m.	p.m.	p.m.	p.m.	p.m.	p.m.
...	...	Lynton	...	7 13	...	9 25		12 42	...	3 30	...	3 40	..	6 12	...	8 5	...	9 30
1	67	Caffyns Halt.................	...	...	9 33	9 33½	12 50	12 50½	3 38	3 38½	3 48	3 48½	6 20	6 20½	8 13	8 13½	9 38	9 38½
3	25	Woody Bay	7 27	7 28	9 40½	9 41½	12 57½	12 58½	3 45½	3 46½	3 55½	3 56½	6 27½	6 29	8 20½	8 21	9 45½	9 47
4	69	Parracombe Halt	7 35	7 35½	9 48½	9 49	1 5½	1 6	3 53½	3 54	4 3½	4 4	6 36	6 37	8 28	8 28½	9 54	9 54½
7	41	Blackmoor....................	7X48½	7 51	10 2	10 4	1 19	1 21	4X 7	4 9	4 17	4 19	6 50	6 52	8 41½	8X42½	10 7½	10 9
11	49	Bratton Fleming............	8 7	8 7½	10 20	10 21	1 37	1 38	4 25	4 26	4 35	4 36	7 8	7 9	8 58½	8 59	1025	1025½
14	48	Chelfham	8 20½	8 21	10X34	10 36½	1X51	1 54	4X39	4 42	4X49	4 52	7 22	7 22½	9 12	9 12½	1038½	1039
16	48	Snapper Halt	8 29½	8 30	10 44½	10 45	2 2	2 2½	5 0	5 1	5 0	5 1	7 30½	7 31	9 20½	9 21	1047	1048
18	73	Barnstaple (Pilton Yard)	8	39	10	54	2E12	2 14	5	10	5	10	7	40	9	30	10	57
19	23	Barnstaple Town	8 41	9†0	10 56	11†10	2 16	2†24	5 12	5†25	5 12	5†25	7 42	...	9 32	9†38	1059	11†5
...	...	Barnstaple (Pilton Yd.)	9†2		11†14	...	2†26	...	5†27	...	5†27	...			9†40	...	11†7	...

A—Runs daily 18th July to 10th September, and Mondays, Wednesdays and Saturdays only, commencing 12th September.
B—Runs 18th July to 10th September only. C—Commencing 12th September start from Pilton Yard 5.35 a.m.
D—Mondays, Wednesdays and Saturdays only commencing 12th September.
E—For exchange of enginemen only.
All services may be utilised for conveying vehicles containing goods traffic or empty goods wagons unless otherwise prohibited.
When goods vehicles are attached to the rear of the train, the last vehicle must be fitted with brake blocks operated by the vacuum brake.

Timing No.	320 (31st JULY, 28th AUGUST and 25th SEPTEMBER only.) Half-Day Excn. from Ilfracombe & Torrington. arr.	dep.	309 (24th JULY, 21st AUGUST and 18th SEPTEMBER only.) Half-Day Excn. from Exmouth. arr.	dep.	310 (17th JULY, 14th AUGUST and 11th SEPTEMBER only.) Half-Day Excn. from Plymouth. C arr.	dep.	318 (7th AUGUST and 4th SEPTEMBER only.) Half-Day Excn. from Bude. C arr.	dep.				
DOWN TRAINS. SUNDAYS.	a.m.	a.m.	p.m.	p.m.	p.m.	p.m.	p.m.	p.m.				
Barnstaple (Pilton Yd.)	...	11†38		12†38		12†48		12†48	...	...	...	...
Barnstaple Town	11†40	11 50	12†40	12 50	12†50	1 C0	12†50	1 C0	...	...	...	...
Barnstaple (Pilton Yard)	11	52	12	52	1	2	1	2	...	...	...	...
Snapper Halt	...	...	...	...	...	...	...	...	...	...	...	...
Chelfham	12	9	1	9	1	19	1	19	...	...	...	...
Bratton Fleming	12	22	1	22	1	32	1	32	...	...	...	...
Blackmoor	12	39	1	39	1	49	1	49	...	...	...	...
Parracombe Halt	...	...	...	...	...	...	...	...	...	...	...	...
Woody Bay	12 59	1 0	1 59	2 0	2 9	2 10	2 9	2 10	...	...	...	...
Caffyns Halt	...		...	...	...		...	...	...	...	...	...
Lynton	1 15	...	2 15	...	2 25	...	2 25	...	...	...	...	...

Timing No.	310 (17th JULY, 14th AUGUST and 11th SEPTEMBER only.) Return Half-Day Excn. to Plymouth. arr.	dep.	318 (7th AUGUST and 4th SEPTEMBER only.) Return Half-Day Excn. to Bude. arr.	dep.			309 (24th JULY, 21st AUGUST and 18th SEPTEMBER only.) Return Half-Day Excn. to Exmouth. arr.	dep.	320 (31st JULY, 28th AUGUST and 25th SEPTEMBER only.) Return Half-Day Excn. to Ilfracombe & Torrington. arr.	dep.		
UP TRAINS. SUNDAYS.	p.m.	p.m.	p.m.	p.m.			p.m.	p.m.	p.m.	p.m.		
Lynton	...	6 30	...	6 30		...		7 30	...	8 10	...	...
Caffyns Halt.................................	...	...	...	...	...	...		...	...	...	...	...
Woody Bay	6 44	6 45	6 44	6 45	...	...	7 44	7 45	8 24	8 25	...	...
Parracombe Halt	...	...	...	...	...	...	...	...	...	...	...	...
Blackmoor....................................	7	5	7	5	...	...	8	5	8	45	...	...
Bratton Fleming	7	20	7	20	...	...	8	20	9	0	...	...
Chelfham	7	32	7	32	...	...	8	32	9	12	...	...
Snapper Halt	...	...	...	...	...	...	...	...	...	...	...	...
Barnstaple (Pilton Yard)............	7	50	7	50	...	...	8	50	9	30	...	...
Barnstaple Town	7 52	8† 0	7 52	8† 0	...	...	8 52	9† 0	9 32	9†40	...	...
Barnstaple (Pilton Yard)............	8† 2	...	8† 2	...	...	...	9† 2		9†43	...	...	...

C—Advertised departure time 12.50 p.m.

'(3) It appears that at least three schemes have been put forward that can be called:- (a) Mr Tucker's scheme (b) The Bottom Meadow route (c) The High Level route via Dyke's Cottage. And to these I must now add a fourth, viz:-(d) The Park Gardens Terrace route.

'(4) I will now shortly describe each route omitting however the first, Mr. Tucker's, as I understand that owing to the opposition of the land owners and the heavy works it has been definitely abandoned. Route B by the Bottom Meadow is practically the route proposed in the Parliamentary plans except that the upper part is carried on beyond the Station site and brought back with a sharp turn so as to ease the gradient. Route C starts from Lee Lane beyond Victoria Nursery, turns up to Dyke's Cottage, and following the contour joins the Shambleway at the top of the hill. Route D starts from the new road at the end of Park Gardens Terrace and passing at the back of Alford Terrace follows the same line as Route C but at a lower level though finishing at the same point.

'(5) The points I have to consider are: (a) Distances from Post Office to Station; (b) Gradient and Total rise; (c) Cost. The question of general efficiency must also be considered though outside the scope of my Report.

'(6) I have taken the Post Office which is just opposite the principal Hotel as my point of Departure as is usually done in such cases.

'(7) The following table shews the figures for each route, B, C and D:

	B	*C*	*D*
Distance from PO to Station...	*1440yd*	*1600yd*	*1265yd*
Length of New Road to make..	*1245yd*	*1135yd*	*800yd*
Ruling Gradient..	*1in10*	*1in15*	*1in10*
Total rise to be overcome..............	*285 ft*	*180ft*	*224ft*
Proportional cost per yard...............	*200*	*100*	*100*
Proportional cost whole Road..........	*311*	*142*	*100*

'(8) In comparing the distances by each route to the Station there is not much difference - Route D is the shortest and Route C the longest, while as regards the amount of new Road to be made, the advantage is decidedly with Route D. 'As regards the total rise Route C is the best and Route B far the worst.

'As regards the gradient Route C has the advantage of being 1 in 15 throughout and Route D is the worst with 1 in 10 throughout, and Route B a bad second with 1 in 9 [sic] and 1 in 10 for about two thirds of its length and 1 in 20 and 1 in 13 for the rest, but the total rise is more than for Route D.

Chelfham station and viaduct, looking towards Barnstaple, early 1930s. Manning Wardle 2-6-2T No 759 YEO comes off the viaduct to enter the station with a Lynton train.

Chelfham viaduct and station, looking towards Lynton, 1906. The station, with its solitary building, is discernible just beyond the far end of the viaduct. The ostentatious pile on the right is Chelfham House.

'As regards the proportional cost Route B is far and away the most inexpensive.

'(9) To sum up the pros and cons for the three routes it appears that the Bottom Meadow route (Route B) is the most costly by far, it has the greatest length to overcome, its gradient is no better than the Park Gardens route (Route D) and it has the longest piece of road to be made new. Indeed I am informed that this will so spoil the bottom meadow itself that the owner refuses to sell part only but will require us to take the whole at a cost of at least £2,000.

'(10) Route C has the advantage of an easy gradient but it is a longer route and requires more new road than Route D, and is perhaps the best for purely Railway purposes as it will be wheel traffic that we have to consider entirely, for I have no doubt that foot passengers will use the shortest route available, viz:- the present Shambleway, whatever be the length or gradient of the new road.

'(11) Everything therefore considered except the wishes of the inhabitants and owners of adjacent property, I am of opinion that either Routes C or D would satisfy the wants and requirements of the Company and that all things else being equal, the road with the lighter gra-

Chelfham station and viaduct, looking towards Barnstaple, 1936. Chelfham station was a passing place with two platforms and a short siding. The semaphore signal at the far end of the viaduct clears the way for a Lynton-bound train.

dient would be best in spite of the extra distance of 335 yards'. After discussions between the L&BR and Lynton District Council., Route C (the Dyke's Cottage route) was indeed adopted, albeit with the railway company's proviso that the final bill was not to exceed £800.

Among the many other pre-opening preliminaries, on 24 February 1897 it was resolved: '*.... that the Board hereby adopt and confirm the provisional arrangement made with Messrs. Evans & O'Donnell & Co Limited for the supply of both Signalling and Telegraph System and apparatus for the whole line and with all extras and to the satisfaction of the Board of Trade for the sum of £2,025'.*

Staffing matters were discussed on 25 February 1898, when it was resolved: '*.... that subject to references R.Fursdon be appointed Station Master at Lynton at 25/- per week wages with quarters, coals and lighting, also uniform consisting of coat, waistcoat, cap and two pairs of trousers per annum .... Henry Lowden be appointed Station Master at Blackmoor at wages of 21/- per week .... Thomas Dewfall be appointed Station Master at Bratton'.*

The official opening of the railway took place on 11 May 1898, public services commencing on 16 May. The initial service comprised five trains each way on weekdays and one on Sundays. Of the weekday trains, the first of the day from Barnstaple (dep. 6.35am) and the last from Lynton (dep. 5.45pm) were intended to carry the mails while the first Lynton to Barnstaple train on weekdays (the 6.14am) was designated a mixed working. Journey times for the 19½ mile trip were around 100 minutes. The fares from Barnstaple, as had

Chelfham station, looking towards Lynton, pre-1923. A minor mystery - the signal post appears to be shorter than that seen in the distance in the 1906 picture (previous page) After the L&B closed, the delightful little station building was sold and converted into a private residence.

Bratton Fleming station, looking towards Lynton, pre-1923. A Barnstaple-bound train, hauled by one of the 2-6-2Ts, enters the station. The first vehicle behind the engine appears to be one of the 4-ton vans. Like the station building at Chelfham, that at Bratton Fleming ultimately became a private dwelling.

Bratton Fleming station, looking towards Lynton, 1906. A handful of passengers await the next train for Barnstaple. The small 'hut' on the Up platform (on the right) is, in fact, the signal cabin. The Down platform was unusual in that it was cut into two by a siding leading into the small goods yard, the siding being clearly visible in the mid-distance.

Bratton Fleming station, looking to- wards Lynton, August 1933. A mixed train, hauled by the 2-6-2T of 1925, No E188 LEW, waits at the station before continuing its journey to Barnstaple.

Bratton Fleming station, looking towards Lynton, August 1933. Although the L&B line was in its final years of life when this picture was taken, it is evident that cosmetic appearances had not been neglected.

Blackmoor station, looking south towards Barnstaple, pre-1923. Once again, the low level of the L&B's platforms is very evident. The barn-like building behind the Down platform (on the left) is the goods shed, the derelict-looking structure half-hidden behind it being the stables, which had been provided in anticipation of a flourishing horse-bus service between here and Ilfracombe. The siding behind the gentleman on the right was removed circa 1930.

been quoted by Sir George Newnes shortly before opening day, were: 1/8d 1st class to Bratton, 2/6d to Blackmoor, 3/4d to Wooda Bay and 4/2d to Lynton. 1st class returns were 2/6d, ‹ ’9d, 5s and 6/3d respectively. 3rd class singles were much less - from Ilfracombe these were 7 1/2d to Bratton, 1s to Blackmoor, 1/4d to Wooda Bay and 1/7 1/2d to Lynton.

The line started at Barnstaple Town station, L&BR trains using the rear of the L&SWR platform; the L&BR's engine shed (a twin-road affair), carriage shed, goods depot and only turntable were at Pilton Yard, to the north of the station. Initially, the intermediate stations were at Chelfham (5 miles from Barnstaple), Bratton - renamed Bratton Fleming in October 1899 - (8 miles), Blackmoor (12 miles) and Wooda Bay - renamed Woody Bay in 1901 - (16 miles). The last-named was some distance from the beauty spot after which it was named, and local entrepreneur Benjamin Green Lake had once proposed a branch from the station to Wooda Bay itself.

Additional stopping places were later provided at Parracombe, in 1899, and Snapper halt in 1903; in 1907 Caffyns halt was opened north of Woody Bay primarily to serve a local golf course. Conversely, an unadvertised workmen's halt at Pilton Yard fell into disuse in 1904.

The station platforms were only some 12in high, and the principal stations were equipped with buildings in the style of Swiss chalets. The most significant engineering feature of the line was Chelfham Viaduct, an impressively slender eight-arch structure which carried the line 70ft above the

66

Blackmoor station, looking north towards Lynton, 1906. In view of its anticipated importance, Blackmoor had one of the more substantial 'Nuremburg'-style station buildings. Nowadays, the building forms the nucleus of a tourist-orientated pub. The structure at the end of the Down platform (on the left) is the pumping house, which housed a hot-air engine to pump the water to the tank above it.

Stoke Rivers Valley. The viaduct cost £6,500 to construct and was built with bricks from the Marland Works of the North Devon Clay Co, to the south-west of Barnstaple.

At the time the railway opened, the L&BR's motive power consisted of three

Manning Wardle 2-6-2Ts. They had been delivered in 1897 in anticipation of the line's completion that year and, in the interim, had been stored at Barnstaple. The locomotives carried Works Nos 1361, 1362 and 1363, and were named YEO, EXE and TAW re-

spectively. In later years the L&BR 2-6-2Ts were often regarded as 'copies' of the famous Davies & Metcalfe 2-6-2Ts which operated on the Vale of Rheidol Railway in Wales, but the L&BR's steeds predated their Welsh counter-parts by five years.

The style of motive power had, in fact, almost been entirely different - witness the Directors' meeting of 22 September 1896: '.... *on report on tenders for locos it was RESOLVED that the tender of the Brush Electrical Engineering Co. be accepted and that three locos be ordered at £800 each to include hand and vacuum brakes according to specifications supplied. The engines to be completed by 31st March 1897 and delivered as required by the Company'.* Confirmation of the swift change of heart is evidenced by a minute of 9 November: *'The Chairman reported that he had inspected locomotives and that the lowest Tender (except that of the Brush Electrical Company) was that of Messrs. Manning & Wardle for £1,100 each for three engines and that subject to the Board's approval he*

Parracombe halt, looking towards Lynton, probably pre-1923. The original timber-built shelter was replaced by a pre-cast concrete example in SR days.

Woody Bay station, looking towards Lynton, 1 June 1935. Originally named Wooda Bay, the station had one of the line's three 'Nuremburg'-style buildings. The starter signal on the Down platform (on the left) appears to be one of the original L&B signals, the other two being decidedly SR in origin.

Woody Bay station, looking towards Barnstaple, early 1930s. The 1 in 50 drop beyond the end of the station looks quite alarming. The headshunt can be seen in the distance (part of it is occupied by a wagon or two), while the start of the short goods siding is discernible immediately beyond the end of the Up platform (on the left).

was delivered in kit form for assembly at the L&BR's workshops. Named LYN, it was first steamed in July 1898.

As for rolling stock, the matter had been discussed by the directors on 9 November 1896: '...an arrangement had been made by the Committee for the purchase of sixteen Passenger Carriages and that the lowest Tender (except that of the Brush Electrical Company) was that of the Bristol Wagon Company Limited at £7,300 less ten per cent'.

The contract for the supply of carriages was duly made with the Bristol Carriage & Wagon Co on 25 January 1897: 'The Rolling Stock shall be in all points fully equipped with lamps, floor cloths, curtains, lamp rests, steps, etcetera, and all other appurtenances necessary. 'The said Rolling Stock shall be completed in all things according to the said plans, diagrams and specifications, and delivered to the Company free on the rails at their Barnstaple Station fit for immediate use by the first day of May 1897. 'The Company (L&BR) shall be entitled to substitute Roller Bearings provided in the said plans .... if such Roller Bearings be supplied by the Company then the sum of Six Pounds shall be deducted for each vehicle. (It appears that roller bearings were indeed used).

SCHEDULE

No.of Veh	Type	Price each
4	Third Class Carriage (ord)	£372.12s
2	Third Class Carriage (with Guard's Cpt)	£393.6s
4	Third Class Carriage (with open Central Compartment)	£372.12s
2	Composite Carriages	£454.10s
2	Composite (with Saloon Compartment)	£505.16s
2	Balcony Vehicles (with Guard's Cpt)	£441.0s

had arranged for same'. Even before the L&BR opened it doors to the public, it was considered that the purchase of a fourth locomotive would be a very useful safeguard. On 25 February 1898 it was resolved: '....that a fourth engine be ordered by the Chairman from Messrs. Manning Wardle & Co or elsewhere as he may think advisable, provided delivery can be obtained by 1 July, otherwise the order be postponed'.

Partly due to the aftermath of a national engineering strike Manning Wardle were unable to supply a fourth locomotive at short notice, and so the order was given, instead, to the Baldwin Locomotive Works of Philadelphia, USA. In order to speed up completion and delivery the L&BR agreed to a 2-4-2T instead of a 2-6-2T, and the locomotive

Caffyns halt, looking towards Lynton, late 1920s. The halt opened in 1907 to serve a nearby golf course. Here, the platform appears to have benefited from fairly recent relaying.

Lynton & Lynmouth station, probably pre-1923. Fittingly, the terminus had one of the larger-style station buildings. It is, incidentally, in use today as holiday accommodation. The goods shed can be seen beyond the end of the loop, but the bay behind the platform is just out of view.

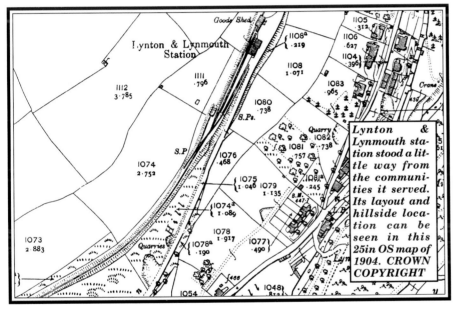

Lynton & Lynmouth station stood a little way from the communities it served. Its layout and hillside location can be seen in this 25in OS map of 1904. CROWN COPYRIGHT

The ordinary third class carriages each had seven compartments and a total of 56 seats, while the composite carriages (without the saloons) comprised two first- and four third-class compartments. The carriages weighed between 81/2 tons and 9 tons each, Sir George Newnes, the L&BR's Chairman stating in *The Railway Magazine* of May 1898 that: *'The first-class carriages are all thoroughly got up in best style, and are upholstered in blue cloth, with maroon-coloured leather in the smoking compartments. The seats are divided to seat three on each side, and luggage-nets are provided, also the usual complement of photographs, mirrors, etc. The third-class carriages are fitted with garden chair-shaped seats, made of alternate slats of white and black woods, and are not upholstered. The*

ordinary third-class carriages have moveable partitions that can be removed in summer so as to leave the carriage open right through .... There are no second-class carriages'.

For freight traffic, the L&BR had a mixture of four-wheeled and bogie vehicles, some open and others closed. The precise totals of freight wagons and their dates of acquisition have been disputed and, mysteriously, the surviving L&BR Minute Books seem unable to shed any light on the matter. However, one source has suggested that there were two wagons on hand for opening day, thirteen more being acquired between 1908 and 1927, and another fourteen later on, while a local rivet-counter has suggested that eighteen freight vehicles were available from the outset.

Despite the great optimism for the L&BR's future, things did not go wholly to plan. As already mentioned, the company had anticipated that much of the road traffic between Ilfracombe and Lynton would be diverted via Blackmoor, with the passengers preferring to travel from there to Lynton by rail. That, however, did not happen, the oft-accepted reason being that the L&BR failed to come up with suitably attractive terms for the proprietors of the horse-buses.

In a bout of lateral thinking, Sir George Newnes purchased a pair of Milnes-Daimler motor-buses in 1903 for an alternative service between Ilfracombe and Blackmoor, but it was unsuccessful. The vehicles were subsequently sold to the GWR and were employed between Helston and The Lizard, in Cornwall.

Somewhat ironically, the L&BR's ally, the L&SWR, later promoted a Bill including a clause which would enable the company to 'carry on road traffic without limitation', and this amused the L&BR not at all. At a meeting on 14 February 1913, the L&BR's directors drafted a letter to their General Manager instructing him to resolve matters: *Referring to the London & South Western Railway Bill of this Session it seems necessary to the Board, as you are aware, that some steps should be taken to come to a common agreement if possible with the South Western Company on such matters as may affect the interests of the Lynton & Barnstaple Railway Company.*

'In this regard, I may draw your attention to the fact that one of the matters seriously affecting the Lynton Railway since its construction has been the question of the road traffic as between Lynton and Blackmoor Gate, so that any alteration of the existing statutory powers and position of the Lynton Company is to be watched with jealous care that nothing should be introduced which might operate to the detriment of that Company.

'On the other hand, our friendly relations with the South Western Company have continued without break or trouble, and the Board at their meeting today have a strong desire to act in a most friendly way with regard to any possible cause of friction which may arise. 'The chief point to which the attention of the Board has been directed is .... that under which the South Western Company may provide, work and use in connection with their system .... road vehicles to be drawn by animal or electrical or mechanical power and convey persons, luggage and goods....

'It appears to the Board that the rights sought may seriously affect the interests of the Lynton Railway Company, even to an extent of giving a locus standi [a place for standing or a right to

Lynton and Lynmouth. Prior to departing for Barnstaple, the driver of No 759 YEO seems intent on being included in the picture. The carriage appears to be one of the four ex-L&B third class observation cars, observation clearly being undertaken from the unglazed centre compartment. PHOTO: B.R. ROBINSON

interfere, according to Chambers 20th Century] *to the South Western Railway in respect of the control of the roads which they may obtain....*

'*....the Board desire that you should see the General Manager of the South Western Railway, and discuss the subject with a view to an undertaking passing between the two Companies that nothing shall be done to affect the Lynton Railway of a prejudicial character'*. The matter was virtually resolved within a week, the L&SWR undertaking to modify the contentious clause in its proposal.

Although not at all relevant to the subject of the L&SWR's proposed bus services, the cordial relationship between the L&BR and the L&SWR is evidenced by a snippet from the minutes of 15 March 1921: '*Reported that: difficulty had been experienced in getting the Manufacturer to execute heavy repairs to a Locomotive Boiler and that arrangements have been made with the London & South Western Railway Company for the work to be carried out at that Company's Works at Eastleigh'*.

Still with irrelevancies, the same minutes included an example of the hazards of rural railway operation: '*Reported: that a colt belonging to Mr.Tucker had broken through the railway fence and had been knocked down and injured by the 6.20am train on February 16th, and that the animal subsequently had to be destroyed and that the owner was claiming £40 in respect of the loss'*.

The L&BR found that its initial estimates of traffic had been a trifle optimistic but the company nevertheless operated at a modest profit for most of its life, the disappointment

concerning the passenger traffic partly offset by a surprisingly healthy quantity of goods. During its peak years, the L&BR carried some 100,000 passengers and around 8,000 tons of goods annually. It is evident that the peak holiday period - which fell in the second half of the year - was critical for the company's financial well-being. However, the peak season in North Devon was frustratingly brief.

The *Western Morning News* of Tuesday 18 March 1913 contained an account of the previous day's half-yearly meeting of the L&BR. It was reported that the Chairman, Sir Thomas Hewitt, had explained that:

'*..... there was a decrease of £52 on passenger traffic, and of that £48 was accounted for by the loss of first class passengers, a loss chiefly attributable to the increased number of motor cars now visiting the North Devon district. Although they* [the L&BR] *carried some 1,600 more third class passengers, mostly at excursion rates, this did not make up for the loss of ordinary first class fares. '.... On the expenditure side the cost of the maintenance and renewal of the permanent way, works etc, showed an increase of £37. More materials, meaning more labour, had been used; and in common with all buyers the Lynton and Barnstaple had to deplore that the cost of supplies had of late increased in an alarming fashion'*.

Also reported was the '*....very sad episode by which two workmen had lost their lives and two others had been more or less injured by the overturning of a trolley in which they were travelling near Chelfham Station'*. The 'trolley' was, in fact, an open ballast wagon which was running by gravity from Bratton Fleming to Chelfham. The accident was the worst

in the L&BR's history.

It has often been suggested that, by the early 1920s, the death of the enthusiastic Sir George Newnes (in 1910) and the retirement of his respected successor, Sir Thomas Hewitt (in 1919) had knocked much of the fight out of the little company. The L&BR was excluded from the master plan of the Grouping, partly because negotiations were already under way for selling out to the L&SWR. It remains unclear (to this writer, at least) just what significant gain the L&SWR hoped to make by acquiring the L&BR so late in the day, but the negotiations continued into 1923 and were ultimately concluded by the newly-formed Southern Railway.

A minute from the L&BR's Directors' meeting of 17 May 1922 had noted: '*Arising out of an informal discussion amongst the Directors present at the Meeting held on March 21st 1921, the Chairman wrote privately to the Chairman of the London & South Western Railway Company respecting the position and future prospects of this Company........*

'*On December 14th the Chairman (L&B Co) attended by Mr Drewett (Secretary and Manager) met the Chairman (General Drummond) and the General Manager (Sir Herbert Walker) of the L&SW Co. The Chairman of the London & SW Co made the following offer for the consideration of the Lynton & Barnstaple Co's Directors with a view to such offer being placed before the Proprietors:*

'*The London & South Western Railway Co -*

(1) To cancel the First Debentures held by them, amounting to £20,000.

(2) To pay to the Lynton & Barnstaple Rly Co £20,000 in cash, the Lynton & Barnstaple Co undertaking not to distribute more than the usual one half per cent on its capital in the way of Dividend for the year 1921'. The sale officially took place on 1 July 1923, the Southern Railway acquiring the L&BR for a total of just £39,000.

The three Manning Wardle 2-6-2Ts, YEO, EXE and TAW became SR Nos E759, E760 and E761 respectively, the Baldwin 2-4-2T LYN becoming No E762. In July 1925 the SR took delivery of a further Manning Wardle 2-6-2T (Works No 2042) built to the same design as the original trio. Costing £2,450, it became No E188 and was named LEW

The SR's outlay on a fifth locomotive was, perhaps, extravagant, but as part of a plucky attempt to boost the fortunes of the L&B line, money was also invested in improvements to the rolling stock (including the acquisition of two mobile cranes, although these were rarely used as re-railing was usually achieved by simpler means), station facilities and the permanent way. However, the perennial problem of seasonal traffic - and a somewhat short season, to boot - and increased competition from road transport were obstacles which could not realistically be overcome. With the benefit of hindsight, it could be asked why the SR didn't attempt to obtain revised powers under the terms of the Light Railways Acts, thereby enabling economies to be made, After all, the SR and, before it, the L&SWR were fairly adept at exploiting provisions in light railway legislation.

Reports of activities on the L&B line featured fairly regularly in the contemporary railway press; this brief (and unconfirmed) report, for example, appeared in *The Railway Magazine* of June 1927: *'The number of coaching vehicles on the line now amounts to 17, and there are 24 goods vehicles. Most of the rolling stock is now painted in the SR colours, the former L&B colours being brown and cream for passenger stock. The trains are made up of varying lengths to meet traffic requirements, and on one occasion noted a down train comprising two bogie coaches hauled by 2-6-2 TAW, pass the up train at Chelfham composed of seven bogie coaches, a four wheeled box van, and a bogie box van, headed by 2-6-2Ts LEW and YEO.*

'A number of LSW-type signals, some with wooden posts and arms, and others with lattice posts and corrugated arms, are in use, although many signals are still of the L&B type .... Signals are provided only for running lines, and there are no distant, siding or other signals'.

The slump of the late 1920s and early 1930s did nothing to help the line's recovery, and the SR eventually decided to call it a day. The last train ran on Sunday 29 September 1935 and, as if to set a precedent for 'pre-closure specials' of later years, two locomotives, YEO and LEW, were required to work double-headed on a packed nine-coach train. Significantly, the 300 or so passengers who rode on that last train far exceeded the number carried in the course of several normal working days.

The old L&B stock was auctioned on 13 November 1935. The five locomotives were knocked down for a total of only £236, while the rolling stock realised between £13. 10s for a first-class coach and £3.15s for an open four-wheel truck. Some of the carriages finished up as rather grandiose garden sheds, but in 1959 one was rescued by the Festiniog Railway for restoration and another was eventually acquired by the National Railway Museum. The turntable at Pilton Yard was sold to the Romney, Hythe & Dymchurch Railway in Kent.

A brief report on ex-L&BR coaches appeared in *The Railway Magazine* of September/October 1942, a correspondent pointing out that two were still on the site of the line. One, a first-class observation coach carrying SR No 6991, was to be seen in an intact but weatherbeaten condition at Snapper Halt, reportedly 'on about 40ft of track', and about 400ft along the route towards Chelfham, composite No 6993 was being used by a local farmer and was, apparently, still in perfect condition. The contributor added that a third coach was to be found at Copplestone, near Exeter.

Of the locomotives, the most junior, LEW, was retained for a time by the SR for the insulting process of dismantling its former stamping ground. After its task was over it was treated to heavy repairs and transported to Swansea, from where it was shipped in September 1936 to Permambuco in Brazil for use on a coffee plantation near Sao Louis. According to the definitive *Locomotives of the Southern Railway* by D.L.Bradley (R C T S), LEW was

reported to have been scrapped in February 1957 after having laid derelict for several years. Over the years, LEW has become something of the Lord Lucan of the railway world as alleged sightings in various parts of the South American continent have been reported with reasonable frequency.

Visitors to North Devon might regard the famous Lynton & Lynmouth Cliff Railway merely as a tourist attraction, but the railway is, in fact, an extremely useful year-round means of transport, well used by the locals. During its long existence, the railway has carried small amounts of goods as well as passengers, and after the terrible floods of 1952, in which 34 people lost their lives, it proved a godsend. From the tourist angle, the railway offers spectacular views across one of the most exquisite bays in North Devon. The cliff railway was the brainchild of Sir George Newnes - the same gentleman who was behind the Lynton & Barnstaple Railway. It opened on 9 April 1890, and during 104 years of operation has carried millions of passengers and has enjoyed an accident-free record. The railway comprises two parallel tracks of 3ft 9in gauge which climb for 862ft on a 1 in 1+ incline. One car operates on each track. The cars are operated by water ballast and are connected by a pair of steel cables, the principle being that, with 700 gallons of water in its tank, the descending car will lift the other car on the counter-balance system. At the point where the two cars pass, the tracks are curved slightly outwards. This can be seen just beyond the bridge in this period view.

Site of Watchet station, looking north, probably circa 1905. This sort of semi-dereliction was familiar throughout the BR network in the mid- and late-1960s, but this picture was taken some sixty years earlier. The old platform of the WSMR is clearly evident on the right, the building on the left being the goods shed (which still stands!). Beyond the level crossing, the railway continued to the Western Pier of the harbour. The line reopened in 1907, but closed again in 1910.

Comberow station, possibly 1907. The WSMRs ex-Metropolitan 4-4-0T waits at Comberow. Hazarding a guess, this picture might have been taken shortly after the reopening of the line in July 1907, the general state of maintenance (or lack of it) to the permanent way and, perhaps the wagonload of debris hinting that things had been quiet for a little while. Note that the engine has been shorn of its condensing apparatus and that the numerals on the chimney seem to have been painted out.

WEST SOMERSET MINERAL RAILWAY

The Brendon Hills, which reach a height of 1,391ft above sea level, lie to the east of Exmoor, the two effectively separated by the upper reaches of the River Exe. The ridge along the top of the Brendon Hills had been mined for iron, it is believed, since Roman times, but larger-scale extraction did not commence until the mid-1800s when new technology was available.

In 1854 the Brendon Hills Iron Ore Co - which had been founded in 1853 by a syndicate of ironmasters based at Ebbw Vale in South Wales - promoted a standard gauge railway as a means of transporting the ore to the harbour at Watchet. Under the banner of the West Somerset Mineral Railway, the line was formally authorised on 16 July 1855 although, somewhat mysteriously, later editions of 'Bradshaw's Shareholders' Guide' gave the date as 27 July 1857. The company's obligatory entry in 'Bradshaw's' (for 1869) noted that its purpose had been '....for making a railway from the Quay, at Watchet, to the parish of Exton, with a branch therefrom. Length of main line, 13 miles; length of branch, 1 furlong .... The line is worked by the Ebbw Vale Company (Limited) for 55 1/4 years' [from 24th June 1864].

The section between Watchet and Roadwater was operational by April 1857, the latter point serving as a temporary railhead for the produce of the mines. Sadly, though, the line's early history was marred by a collision between two locomotives (a pair of diminutive outside-cylindered Neilson 0-4-0STs) at Kentsford (near Watchet) in August 1857, three men being killed and one of the locomotives subsequently being scrapped.

The line was extended to Comberow by December 1857, but its major obstacle lay ahead. The mines themselves were stretched out along the ridge some 800ft above Comberow, and so a massive incline had to be constructed. The rope-worked incline was some three quarters of a mile long and on a gradient of 1 in 4, but although it was ready for action by May 1858 it was operated by a stationary engine until a permanent engine house was completed in March 1861. From the top of the incline, two branches eventually extended along the hills. One ran four miles westwards to Gupworthy (the original intention having been to reach Heath Poult), and the other extended eastwards for just half a mile to Raleigh's Cross mine.

At Watchet, the much neglected harbour was entrusted to a board of commissioners on which the iron ore company was well represented. The new administration ordered the dredging of the quays and approaches, and also the reconstruction of the West Pier for the anticipated traffic from the mines.

Inevitably, small mining communities were established in the Brendon Hills area, and so the WSMR introduced a public passenger service between Watchet and Comberow. The service was inaugurated on 1 September 1865, trains calling at the two intermediate stations at Washford and Roadwater. On the section at the top of the incline, basic stations were provided at Brendon Hill, Gupworthy and Luxborough Road, but they were not treated to an official passenger service. The formidable incline was, predictably, designated a passenger-free zone, but the WSMR seemed quite willing to carry passengers on the incline in an open truck although, mindful of the legalities, the company emphasised that these journeys were free of charge and most definitely at the passengers' own risk.

For the record, the public timetables of 1874 listed four passenger services each way between Watchet and Comberow on weekdays and an additional working early on Saturday evenings. Journey times for the six-mile trip were between 30 and 40 minutes, the fares for the whole journey being a shilling first class, 9d second class and 6d third class. As the railway was geared to serve the mining communities, one can only speculate as to how heavily the first- and second-class accommodation was used.

In the mid-1870s the combined effects of a recession in the iron trade and the import of cheap Spanish ore proved disastrous for the Brendon Hill mines, and production ceased in May 1879. Although the combined output of the mines had peaked at 47,000 tons in 1877, the price of the ore that year was only 14/- per ton - some 6/- down on the price a few years earlier. Nevertheless, mining was resumed a few months later, but continued only until 1883. Despite the economic blow to the area the WSMR continued to operate a public passenger service, usually of two trains each way on weekdays.

In the early 1890s the railway company sought to keep its expenditure down to the bare minimum by requesting exemption from legislation regard-

Roadwater station, 3 July 1907. For the reopening of the line by the Somerset Mineral Syndicate, Beyer Peacock 4-4-0T No 37 was purchased from the Metropolitan Railway. The day before the official reopening, the engine and one truck made the journey from Watchet to Roadwater, the arrival being duly recorded for posterity. PHOTO: DR G. COURT COLLECTION

WEST SOMERSET MINERAL.

DIRECTORS:

William Gregory Norris, Esq., Coalbrook- | Joseph Brailsford, Esq., York Street, dale, Salop. | Sheffield.
John Henry Robinson, Esq., 13, Victoria Street, London.

OFFICERS.—Sec. and Solicitor, Edwin Hellard, Stogumber, Taunton ; Auditors, Edwin Grove and Joseph Coventry. Bankers, Stuckey's Banking Co., Taunton.

Incorporated by act of 27th July, 1857, for making a railway from the Quay, at Watchet, to the parish of Exton, with a branch therefrom. For details of this Act, see MANUAL for 1907, page 355.

This line was worked by the Ebbw Vale Steel, Iron, and Coal Company Limited, for 55¼ years, from 24th June, 1864, that company guaranteeing interest on the mortgages and debenture stock, 6 per cent. on the "A" and 5 per cent. on the "B" shares. The line of 11½ miles was worked at a loss for some years, and the West Somerset Company agreed, subject to the guarantee being paid, to the request of the Ebbw Vale Company to be relieved of its liability to carry on the traffic, which has consequently been stopped.

CAPITAL.—The expenditure, including loan of 10,000*l*. to Watchet Harbour, has amounted to 111,774*l*., and the receipts, amounting to the same sum, included 32,500*l*. in perpetual 6 per cent. preference class "A" shares, 42,500*l*. in class "B" (ordinary) shares, 13,700*l*. on loan, and 16,300*l*. in debenture stock.

Meetings held in February or March and in August or September in each year.

No. of Directors—5; minimum, 3; quorum, 3. *Qualification*, 500*l*.

Brendon Hills, circa 1907. For the reopening of the WSMR in 1907, a 2ft gauge line was laid between the top of the incline and Colton. It was worked by a Kerr Stuart 0-4-0T and, the subject here, a Bagnall 0-4-0WT. PHOTO: DR G. COURT COLLECTION

ing the use of continuous brakes, the block system, and interlocking signals, as had been prescribed by the Regulation of Railways Act of 1889. Correspondence bounced back and forth between the WSMR offices at Stogumber and the Board of Trade.

A plea from Mr Edwin Hellard, the WSMR's secretary and solicitor, 14 February 1890: *'The line is a single line with only one Engine upon it, and therefore I gathered from your letter of 24 October last that no such order is required. The company runs only two carriages and the engine and one carriage have breaks.(sic) There are sometimes a few small trucks attached, but the traffic is very small...'*

From Albert Horne, the WSMR's engineer, 12 March 1891: *'The working of this Railway has been carried on in a way (herein) explained since its construc-*

tion nearly 30 years ago - and during that period there have been no instances of any defect in the working arrangements referred to. [Not altogether true, as accidents were not exactly unknown]. *The Traffic on the line is small and at a speed of only 12 miles per hour. I am of the opinion that the present system is perfectly safe, and I hope the Board of Trade will, under the circumstances, be satisfied that it is unnecessary to make the alterations stipulated in the order referred to'.*

The Board of Trade's response of 9 June 1891 included a copy of the very report which had been supplied by the WSMR three months previously: *'Report on the present system of working the (WSM) Ry, with observation on an order issued by the Board of Trade in reference (firstly) to the Block system, (secondly) to the interlocking of points and signals, and (thirdly) to the Brake power employed thereon.*

'Block System. The railway from Watchet to Comberow is about six miles in length, having four stations thereon, at which every train stops, the annexed Time Bill shows that the distance each way is run in half an hour, - including stoppages, or at a speed of about 12 miles an hour, one engine only is used, the train being usually made up of Engine, two Carriages and sometimes with trucks of minerals; there is no telegraph on the line, and practically it is now worked on the 'Block System', one train only being on the line at the same time. The present mode of working is by 'distant' signals at the several stations which are under the entire charge of the station masters.

'Interlocking of Points. The sidings, of which there are five, are also under the charge of the station masters, the points are kept locked being operated only when a truck has to be left or taken on.

'Brake Power. The Brakes used on the wheels of the engine, carriages and trucks

Brendon Hill incline, 24 July 1907. Although the WSMR's reopening took place on 4 July 1907, traffic did not start to use the incline until 17 July. This picture of a truck arriving at the top of the incline was taken a week later. PHOTO: DR G. COURT COLLECTION

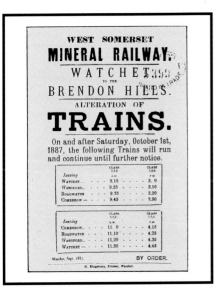

are of the ordinary wooden concave pattern, of a durable nature which can be applied instantaneously, by the Engine Driver to the Engine and by the Guard to the Carriages.'

It appears that a mutually acceptable suggestion subsequently appeared on the horizon. From the WSMR, 30 September 1891: *'...as per the Board of Trade request .... we the WSMR Co hereby undertake that the line from Watchet Station to Comberow Station shall be worked by one Engine in steam (or two coupled together) at one and the same time, such Engine or Engines to carry a staff'.*

Things were not, however, resolved quite so readily, one suggestion being that the WSMR conveniently 'forgot' that it had not been exempted from the regulations. From Major Yorke (for the Board of Trade), 14 August 1894: *'I have inspected the West Somerset Mineral Railway .... The line is in a very unsatisfactory condition and the requirements of the order made upon the company as regards interlocking have not been complied with.*

'The whole of the points throughout the line are worked by single hand levers, which are locked by ordinary galvanised iron padlocks of the same pattern as those in use at the level crossing gates, and although one padlock key is attached by a ring and staple to the train staff, there are several other keys in the possession of the station masters and gatekeepers, each of which is capable of unlocking any of the siding points - the points are in no case provided with facing point locks, and there are no safety catch points on any of the sidings at their junctions with the passenger line.

'At Comberow on the steep incline outside the station there are runaway catch points on the passenger line, which are worked by a single hand lever and locked up in their cases - and the arrangement of the sidings at this place is decidedly

faulty, there being no loop to enable the engine to get round its train, and a great deal of shunting being therefore necessary on the single line.

'The line is on a steep rising gradient the whole way from Watchet to Comberow, and none of the precautions usual on single lines can be safely dispensed with.

'The company should be called upon to provide forthwith:
(1) Safety catch points on all sidings at the junctions of the latter with the main line.
(2) Facing point locks at all points which are at any time facing points to passenger trains (one of the economical forms of point lock, whereby one lever works both the points and the bolts, would be sufficient).
(3) A proper Annetts Key permanently attached to and forming an integral part of the train staff.
(4) A proper loop and sidings at Comberow so that the catch point on the single line outside the station can be removed, and all shunting done with engine at the Watchet end of the train, and the sidings, being as before stated, provided with safety points.
The whole of the above works should be completed within three months.

'As regards continuous brakes, the company have recently purchased two coaches which are provided with the vacuum automatic brake, and the engine is to be fitted with the vacuum brake apparatus immediately'. It seems that the WSMR finally complied, as the Board of Trade gave its approval in December 1894.

A trifle ironically, though, all traffic on the line ceased only four years later, on 7 November 1898. After closure, the surviving rolling stock was evacuated either to Ebbw Vale or to a Newport scrapyard via a temporary link with the

GWR's Minehead branch at Kentsford. During its 41-year life the WSMR had used eight different locomotives, although three seem to have been only short-term replacements when the regular engines had been out of action. They had all been Neilson 0-4-0STs or Sharp Stewart 0-6-0STs, one of each type being there at the end. The Sharp Stewart representative, named PONTYPOOL, had been delivered new in 1866 to work the Watchet - Comberow section, the Neilson engine having been transferred from Ebbw Vale as late as 1896 for use on the section above the incline. The company's engine shed was at Watchet.

Despite the cessation of traffic on the WSMR in 1898, that was not the very end for the railway. In 1907 the Somerset Mineral Syndicate was formed to reopen some of the mines, and took a lease on the still-intact railway. Motive power was provided by a Beyer Peacock 4-4-0T which had been bought from the Metropolitan Railway, that engine (MR No 37) having been one of many displaced by the spread of electrification. The line was ceremonially reopened on 4 July 1907 but, despite the arrival of three second-hand carriages, it is believed that no scheduled passenger services were advertised. The celebrated incline was reopened and a 2ft-gauge locomotive-worked line was laid between the top and workings at Colton, although the other sections of the hill-top line remained closed. Despite the new-found optimism, the reprieve was brief as the venture collapsed in March 1910, the locomotives and rolling stock being auctioned a couple of months later.

Tenacious to the end, the old mineral line was not yet ready to fade com-

Brendon Hill incline, 24 July 1907. Another 'week-after-reopening' picture, this time of a truck starting its descent down the incline. Note the semaphore signal, and also the legend on the wagon - Bristol Carriage & Wagon Works. PHOTO: DR G. COURT COLLECTION

pletely into obscurity. Between 1911 and 1914 the section between Watchet and Washford was used as a demonstration track for the Australian engineer, A.R. Angus, who wished to show off his new method of automatic train control. Two GWR 2-4-0s, Nos 212 and 213, took part in the ATC tests, the locomotives having gained access to the WSMR line by means of the reinstated 'temporary' link at Kentsford. It seems that the demonstrations were successful, as the two driverless locomotives were set off from the opposite ends of the line and, much to the chagrin of the ghouls in the crowd, pulled up automatically some 200yd apart.

After Mr Angus had removed his paraphernalia, the West Somerset Mineral Railway was finally left to rust in peace. The rails were requisitioned by the War Department in 1917 (although not all were removed until after the war), and on 2 August 1923 the railway's proprietor, the Brendon Hills Iron Ore Co, was formally wound up.

Throughout its life, the WSMR was devoid of any permanent physical connection with the outside world. There had once been speculation that the Bristol & Exeter Railway would try to take it over and, prior to that, in 1857 the WSMR had itself obtained authorisation for an extension to Minehead. But, of course, neither happened. Throughout Britain, there are countless examples of small railway companies which have long since passed into oblivion, but the West Somerset Mineral Railway must, surely, be one of the most unsung of all.

Today, many remnants of the line are still clearly distinguishable. For example, the daunting incline leading to Brendon Hill is identifiable from alongside the unclassified Elworthy - Wheddon Cross road, and the site of Watchet station remains largely undeveloped. Furthermore, parts of the trackbed are clearly visible either side of Watchet, and can be seen from the trains on the preserved Taunton - Minehead line. Watchet itself is a very pleasant little town, and its small museum has a worthwhile collection of archive photographs of what was known to locals as 'the old mineral line'.

Brendon Hill incline, looking north, circa 1908. This view down the incline shows Comberow station at the bottom, the ex-Met 4-4-0T taking on water to the left of the station itself.

Bottom right:- Brendon Hill incline, looking south, 4 July 1907. A public excursion was run on reopening day, passengers being conveyed in open trucks. This was the scene at Comberow, a number of the passengers evidently taking the opportunity of walking up the incline. As previously stated, the incline was not reopened until 17 July, and this picture clearly shows the still-herbaceous state of parts of the incline and its approach.